Franz
LISZT

MAZEPPA

Symphonic Poem No. 6

S. 100

Study Score
Partitur

PETRUCCI LIBRARY PRESS

INTRODUCTION

The present score is a reissue of one from the Franz Liszt-Stiftung edition, originally published by Breitkopf & Härtel from 1907-1936. The edition was prepared in an effort to publish the entire oeuvre of Franz Liszt. Editors included such prominent musicians as Béla Bartok, Ferruccio Busoni, Eugène d'Albert and José Vianna da Motta – some of whom studied with Liszt – as well as scholars like Peter Raabe, who would later compile the first catalog of the composer's works. The need for a complete edition was already apparent by the time of Liszt's death. Although some of his piano music had regularly appeared in new editions throughout his life, these works were by no means representative of even his pianistic output. A far more unfortunate fate was left for his orchestral music - which would usually be issued only once, soon to go out of print and later scarcely available. The Liszt-Stiftung edition revived many works that had fallen into relative obscurity and was therefore handsomely welcomed.

The edition was sadly never completed. The publication activity was brought to a premature end by the time of the Second World War. All in all the incomplete edition encompassed 34 volumes, among others two symphonies, the symphonic poems, some concert works, a couple of piano arrangements and 11 volumes of original works for piano – a mere fraction of the composer's output – but the edition would nonetheless break the ground for Liszt research during the 20th century for a number of reasons. First, it brought to light a number of late pieces that would put Liszt as a forerunner of experimental music and firmly establish his position as such. Second, it revealed the diversity of Liszt's output, which up until that time had been best known as an important addition to the piano repertoire. Third, it displayed the complex and characteristic nature of many of his works by being the first edition to show and make use of several alternative (sometimes vastly different) versions and sources. Last but not least, it would provide the world with a generally reliable edition of easy availability and very high standard for its day.

The Bavarian State Library acquired a complete copy of said edition and decided to digitize it in 2008. By that time more than 70 years had passed since its publication, effectively rendering the edition out of copyright and free for any use. Each and every page was scanned and uploaded to their online digital collection. While this was a great effort in itself, the site has a rudimentary interface, is difficult to navigate and the scores are not in the context of relevant information. One of our users decided to also upload it to our site, the International Music Score Library Project (IMSLP) / Petrucci Music Library, the unique wiki-based repository of musical scores, composers and indexes that anyone can edit and amend. Through the effort of a single user, Mattias K. (piupianissimo), the entire edition is now easily available worldwide to those who wish to perform and study the composer's music in a historical context, since as the case is with Liszt's music, many early editions exist and many are readily available on the site and many more will be available in the future. IMSLP is as such a valuable resource available to the scholar but even more to the performer who is always a mere mouse click away from scores that have not been in print since the turn of the past century, or that are otherwise hard to come by. The availability, quantity of ease of access for online scores will soon exceed those of the traditional medium of print. Nevertheless new works have always been published through the printed medium and this tradition is going to persist for many years to come even if complemented by the digital medium. Of course an important fact to stress is that the availability of digital scores online does not exclude the need of printed score since neither one can replace the comfort and neatness of one another. The quality of a bound reprint or new engraving exceeds that of a score printed at home.

I discovered IMSLP back in early 2006 when it first began. At that time many scores were scattered on the net either privately or on commercial collection sites. Many of these sites had a considerably large collection but sadly many had restrictions on number of downloads per day and the process of contributing to them was riddled with bureaucracy. IMSLP was the first free site where anyone could contribute and upload any kind of musical scores. I have personally searched and uploaded many works – particularly those of Liszt – and the future of the site is nothing but bright. At the time of its start only a handful of scores were available on the site but through the effort of its users IMSLP has grown to be the largest collection of scores available on the Internet.

Mazeppa is the sixth work in a series of thirteen symphonic poems composed by Franz Liszt. It was composed from 1851-54 and first published in 1856 by Breitkopf und Härtel of Leipzig. The dedicatee is Princess Carolyne zu Sayn-Wittgenstein. This score is from the third volume of the Franz Liszt-Stiftung edition, edited by Otto Taubmann and published in 1909. The score, along with a number or arrangements, is also available directly at the following URL:
http:// imslp.org/wiki/Mazeppa,_S.100_(Liszt,_Franz)

Soren Afshar (Funper)
Summer, 2011

COMPOSER'S PREFACE

Eine Aufführung, welche den Intentionen des Komponisten entsprechen und ihnen Klang, Farbe, Rhythmus und Leben verleihen soll, wird bei meinen Orchester-Werken am zweckmässigsten und mit dem geringsten Zeitverlust durch geteilte Vor-Proben gefördert werden. Demzufolge erlaube ich mir, die HH. Dirigenten, welche meine symphonischen Dichtungen aufzuführen beabsichtigen, zu ersuchen, der General-Probe Separat-Proben mit dem Streich-Quartett, andere mit Blas- und Schlag-Instrumenten vorangehen zu lassen.

Gleichzeitig sei mir gestattet zu bemerken, dass ich das mechanische, taktmässige, zerschnittene Auf- und Abspielen, wie es an manchen Orten noch üblich ist, möglichst beseitigt wünsche, und nur den periodischen Vortrag, mit dem Hervortreten der besonderen Accente und der Abrundung der melodischen und rhythmischen Nuanzierung, als sachgemäss anerkennen kann. In der geistigen Auffassung des Dirigenten liegt der Lebensnerv einer symphonischen Produktion, vorausgesetzt, dass im Orchester die geziemenden Mittel zu deren Verwirklichung sich vorfinden; andernfalls möchte es ratsamer erscheinen, sich nicht mit Werken zu befassen, welche keineswegs eine Alltags-Popularität beanspruchen.

Obschon ich bemüht war, durch genaue Anzeichnungen meine Intentionen zu verdeutlichen, so verhehle ich doch nicht, dass Manches, ja sogar das Wesentlichste, sich nicht zu Papier bringen lässt, und nur durch das künstlerische Vermögen, durch sympathisch schwungvolles Reproduzieren, sowohl des Dirigenten als der Aufführenden, zur durchgreifenden Wirkung gelangen kann. Dem Wohlwollen meiner Kunstgenossen sei es daher überlassen, das Meiste und Vorzüglichste an meinen Werken zu vollbringen.

Weimar, März 1856.

Pour obtenir un résultat d'exécution correspondant aux intentions de mes œuvres orchestrales, et leur donner le coloris, le rhythme, l'accent et la vie qu'elles réclament, il sera utile d'en préparer la répétition générale par des répétitions partielles des instruments à cordes, à vent, en cuivre, et à percussion. Par cette méthode de la division du travail on épargnera du temps en facilitant aux exécutants l'intelligence de l'ouvrage. Je me permets en conséquence de prier MM. les chefs d'orchestre qui seraient disposés à faire exécuter l'un de ces Poèmes symphoniques, de vouloir bien prendre le soin de faire précéder les répétitions générales, des répétitions préalables indiquées ci-dessus.

En même temps j'observerai que la mesure dans les œuvres de ce genre demande à être maniée avec plus de mesure, de souplesse, et d'intelligence des effets de coloris, de rhythme, et d'expression qu'il n'est encore d'usage dans beaucoup d'orchestres. Il ne suffit pas qu'une composition soit régulièrement bâtonnée et machinalement exécutée avec plus ou moins de correction pour que l'auteur ait à se louer de cette façon de propagation de son œuvre, et puisse y reconnaître une fidèle interprétation de sa pensée. Le nerf vital d'une belle exécution symphonique gît principalement dans la compréhension de l'œuvre reproduite, que le chef d'orchestre doit surtout posséder et communiquer, dans la manière de partager et d'accentuer les périodes, d'accuser les contrastes tout en ménageant les transitions de veiller tantôt à établir l'équilibre entre les divers instruments, tantôt à les faire ressortir soit isolément soit par groupes, car à tel moment il convient d'entonner ou de marquer simplement les notes, mais à d'autres il s'agit de phraser, de chanter, et même de déclamer. C'est au chef qu'il appartient d'indiquer à chacun des membres de l'orchestre la signification du rôle qu'il a à remplir.

Je me suis attaché à rendre mes intentions par rapport aux nuances, à l'accélération et au retard des mouvements, etc. aussi sensibles que possible par un emploi détaillé des signes et des expressions usitées; néanmoins ce serait une illusion de croire qu'on puisse fixer sur le papier ce qui fait la beauté et le caractère de l'exécution. Le talent et l'inspiration des artistes dirigeants et exécutants en ont seuls le secret, et la part de sympathie que ceux-ci voudront bien accorder à mes œuvres, seront pour elles le meilleur gage de succès.

Weimar, Mars 1856.

In order to secure a performance of my orchestral works which accords with their intentions, and which imparts to them the colour, rhythm, accent and life that they require, it is recommended that the general rehearsal should be preceded by separate rehearsals of the Strings, Wind, Brass, and instruments of percussion. By this division of labour time will be saved, and the executants will more rapidly be made familiar with what is required of them. I therefore venture to request that conductors, who are pleased to bring one or the other of my symphonic poems to a hearing will adopt the plan formulated above.

At the same time I may be allowed to remark that it is my wish that the mechanical, bar by bar, up and down beating of time, which obtains in so many places, should as far as possible be discarded, and that only the periodic divisions, with the prominence of certain accentuation and the rounding off of melodic and rhythmical nuances should alone be regarded as indispensable. The vitality of a symphonic performance depends upon the intellectual perception of the conductor, presuming that suitable material for its realisation is to be found in the orchestra; failing this it would seem to be advisable to hold aloof from works which do not claim a promise of every-day popularity.

Although I have endeavoured to make my intentions clear by providing exact marks of expression, I cannot conceal from myself that much, and that perhaps the most important, cannot be set forth on paper, but can only be successfully brought to light by the artistic capability and the sympathetic and enthusiastic reproduction by both conductor and executants. It may therefore be left to my colleagues in art to do the most and best that they can for my works.

Weimar. March 1856.

F. Liszt.

MAZEPPA.

SYMPHONISCHE DICHTUNG No. 6 VON F. LISZT.

Away! away!
Byron, Mazeppa.

I.

Wie sie Mazeppa trotz Knirschen und Toben,
Gebunden an allen Gliedern, gehoben
Auf das schnaubende Ross,
Dem glühend die weiten Nüstern dampften,
Dess Hufen den bebenden Boden stampften,
Dass er Funken ergoss;

Wie schlangengleich er in Banden gerungen,
Dass rings Gelächter schallend erklungen
Seiner Henker im Chor,
Bis widerstandlos ihn die Fessel zwinget,
Und Schaum vom Munde, Blut ihm dringet
Aus den Augen hervor:

Da gellt ein Schrei, und schneller als Pfeile
Fliegt mit dem Mann in rasender Eile
In die Weite das Ross:
Staubwirbel hüllet die Atemlosen,
Der Wolke gleich, darin Donner tosen
Und der Blitze Geschoss.

Sie flieh'n; sie fliegen durch Talesengen
Wie Stürme, die zwischen Bergen sich drängen,
Wie der fallende Stern;
Nun sind sie ein schwärzlicher Punkt noch zu
sehen,
Bis sie wie Schaum auf der Welle zergehen
An dem Horizont fern.

Sie flieh'n; in die unermesslichen, wilden
Oeden, wo endlos sich Kreise bilden
Immer neu, immer mehr;
Ihr Ritt ist ein Flug, und die Türm' und Städte
Und Bäume und riesiger Berge Kette
Tanzen wild um sie her.

Und wenn der Gebund'ne im Krampf sich rühret,
Dann sprengt das Ross wie vom Sturm entführet,
Immer jäher erschreckt,
In die Wildniss, die kahlen, unwohnlichen Steppen,
Wo das Land mit faltigen Sandesschleppen
Wie ein Mantel sich streckt.

Rings Alles in düstren Farben brennet,
Es rennt der Wald, die Wolke rennet
Ihm vorbei, und der Turm
Und der Berg in rötliches Licht sich tauchend,
Und hinter ihm Rosse, die schnaubend und rauchend
Galoppieren im Sturm.

Und hoch der abendlich strahlende Bogen,
Der Ozean, der aus den Wolkenwogen
Neue Wolken entrollt!
Die Sonne, eh' ihm die Sinne vergehen,
Sieht er, ein marmornes Rad, sich drehen,
Mit Geäder von Gold.

MAZEPPA.

POÈME SYMPHONIQUE No. 6 DE F. LISZT.

Away! — Away! —
Byron, Mazeppa.
En avant! En avant!

I.

Ainsi, quand Mazeppa, qui rugit et qui pleure,
A vu ses bras, ses pieds, ses flancs qu'un sabre
effleure,
Tous ses membres liés
Sur un fougueux cheval, nourri d'herbes marines
Qui fume, et fait jaillir le feu de ses narines
Et le feu de ses pieds;

Quand il s'est dans ses nœuds roulé comme un
reptile,
Qu'il a bien réjoui de sa rage inutile
Ses bourreaux tout joyeux,
Et qu'il retombe enfin sur la croupe farouche,
La sueur sur le front, l'écume dans la bouche,
Et du sang dans les yeux:

Un cri part, et soudain voilà que dans la plaine
Et l'homme et le cheval, emportés, hors d'haleine,
Sur les sables mouvants,
Seuls, emplissant de bruit un tourbillon de poudre,
Pareil au noir nuage où serpente la foudre,
Volant avec les vents!

Ils vont. Dans les vallons comme un orage ils
passent,
Comme ces ouragans qui dans les monts s'en-
tassent,
Comme un globe de feu;
Puis déjà ne sont plus qu'un point noir dans
la brume.
Puis s'effacent dans l'air comme un flocon d'écume
Au vaste océan bleu.

Ils vont. L'espace est grand. Dans le désert
immense,
Dans l'horizon sans fin qui toujours recommence.
Ils se plongent tous deux.
Leur course comme un vol les emporte, et
grands chênes,
Villes et tours, monts noirs liés en longues chaînes,
Tout chancelle autour d'eux.

Et si l'infortuné, dont la tête se brise,
Se débat, le cheval, qui devance la brise,
D'un bond plus effrayé
S'enfonce au désert vaste, aride, infranchissable,
Qui devant eux s'étend, avec ses plis de sable
Comme un manteau rayé.

Tout vacille et se peint de couleurs inconnues,
Il voit courir les bois, courir les larges nues,
Le vieux donjon détruit,
Les monts dont un rayon baigne les intervalles;
Il voit; et des troupeaux de fumantes cavales
Le suivent à grand bruit!

Et le ciel, où déjà les pas du soir s'allongent,
Avec ses océans de nuages où plongent
Des nuages encor,
Et son soleil qui fend leurs vagues de sa proue,
Sur son front ébloui tourne comme une roue
De marbre aux veines d'or!

MAZEPPA.

SYMPHONIC POEM No. 6 BY F. LISZT.

Away! — Away! —
Byron, Mazeppa.

I.

Behold this Mazeppa, o'erpowered by minions,
Writhe vainly beneath the implacable pinions
His limbs that surround.
To a fiery steed from the Asian mosses
That, chafing and fuming, its mane wildly tosses,
The victim is bound.

He turns in the toils like a serpent in madness,
And when his tormentors have feasted in gladness
Upon his despair,
When bound to his sinister saddle, poor creature,
With brow dropping sweat and with foam on
each feature
His eyes redly glare:

A shout — and the unwilling centaur is hieing,
The flight of the steeds of Apollo outvieing,
O'er mountain and plain;
The sand cloud behind him e'er deep'ning and
height'ning,
The track of a storm pierced by flashes of lightning;
A mad hurricane.

They fly. Helter-skelter they rush through the
valley,
Like tempests that out of rock fastnesses sally,
Or levin's dread flash;
Then faded in mist to a speck without motion,
Then melted away like the froth of the ocean
That wild breakers dash.

They fly. Empty space is behind and before them;
The boundless horizon, the sky arching o'er them,
They plunge ever through:
Their feet are like wings. See the forest, the
fountain,
The village, the castle, the long chain of
mountain
All reel on the view!

And if the poor wretch in unconscious convulsion
But struggle, the horse with a fiercer impulsion
Outstripping the blast,
Dashes into a desert vast, trackless, and arid,
Extending before them, a sand plain unvaried,
Earth's mantle so vast.

Strange colours the wavering landscape is wearing;
The forest, the cloud-castles, madly go tearing,
And whirl on their base.
The peaks where the sunbeam a passage just forces
He sees; the next moment a herd of wild horses
Gives noisily chase.

O the sky, where night's footsteps already are
nearing!
Its oceans of cloud with yet more clouds appearing
To melt in their hold;
The sun with its sharp prow dividing those billows
Which turn at its glorious touch into pillows
Of satin and gold.

Dann dunkelt sein Blick, sein Haupthaar hänget
Hernieder straff, sein Blut besprenget
　　Das Gestrüpp und den Sand,
Ihm schwillt der Leib im umwindenden Strange,
Der ihn, wie gierig ihr Opfer die Schlange
　　Immer enger umwand.

Und rasender immer tobt und schiesset
Das Ross dahin, dem Blut entfliesset
　　Aus zerrissenem Fleisch;
Und weh! schon mengt in der Rosse Traben,
Das dumpf dahinbraust, ein Zug von Raben
　　Sein unheimlich Gekreisch'.

Es kommen die Raben, und hoch in Lüften
Der Aar, verscheuchet von Modergrüften,
　　Es vermehren den Schwarm
Die Eulen, der Geier, der mästend auf Leichen
Taucht mit dem Hals in modernde Weichen
　　Wie mit nackendem Arm.

Ihr Nest verlassend im nächt'gen Fluge
Gesellen sie sich dem Leichenzuge,
　　Der die Lüfte durchschnellt;
Mazeppa, sinnlos, hört nicht ihr Toben,
Er starrt nach dem riesigen Fächer nur oben,
　　Wessen Hand ihn wohl hält?

Sternlos die Nacht! die geflügelte Meute
Folgt gierig, rastlos, der sichren Beute,
　　Bis sie fiel und erlag;
Er sieht nur ein wirbelndes, düstres Gewirre,
Und hört wie im Traum nur im dumpfen Ge-
　　　　　　schwirre
　　Ihrer Fittiche Schlag.

Und nach dem rasenden Ritt dreier Tage,
Der sie durch Wüsten, Steppen und Hage
　　Ueber Eisbrücken trug,
Hinstürzt das Ross bei der Vögel Rufe,
Es löschen die Blitze, die mit dem Hufe
　　Aus den Steinen es schlug.

Da liegt er niedergeschmettert und glühet
Vom Blute röter, als Ahorn blühet
　　Wenn der Lenz ihn belaubt;
Der Vögel Wolke kreiset, die graue,
Begierig harret manch' scharfe Klaue
　　Zu zerfleischen sein Haupt.

Und doch! der sich windet im Staub und ächzt,
Der lebende Leichnam von Raben umkrächzet,
　　Wird ein Herrscher, ein Held!
Als Herr der Ukraine einst wird er streiten,
Und reichliche Mahlzeit den Geiern bereiten
　　Auf dem blutigen Feld.

Ihm blühet Grösse aus Qual und Leiden,
Der Mantel der Hetmans wird ihn umkleiden,
　　Dass ihm Alles sich neigt;
Der Zelte Volk wird sich huldigend scharen
Um seinen Thron, ihn begrüssen Fanfaren,
　　Wenn er herrlich sich zeigt.

Son œil s'égare et luit, sa chevelure traîne,
Sa tête pend; son sang rougit la jaune arène,
　　Les buissons épineux:
Sur ses membres gonflés la corde se replie,
Et comme un long serpent resserre et multiplie
　　Sa morsure et ses nœuds.

Le cheval, qui ne sent ni le mors ni la selle,
Toujours fuit, et toujours son sang coule et
　　　　ruisselle,
　　Sa chair tombe en lambeaux;
Hélas! voici déjà qu'aux cavales ardentes
Qui le suivaient, dressant leurs crinières pendantes
　　Succèdent les corbeaux!

Les corbeaux, le grand-duc à l'œil rond qui
　　　　s'effraie,
L'aigle effaré des champs de bataille, et l'orfraie
　　Monstre au jour inconnu,
Les obliques hiboux, et le grand vautour fauve
Qui fouille au flanc des morts où son col rouge
　　　　et chauve
　　Plonge comme un bras nu!

Tous viennent élargir la funèbre volée!
Tous quittent pour le suivre et l'yeuse isolée,
　　Et les nids du manoir.
Lui, sanglant, éperdu, sourd à leurs cris de joie,
Demande en les voyant qui donc là-haut déploie
　　Ce grand éventail noir.

La nuit descend lugubre, et sans robe étoilée.
L'essaim s'acharne, et suit, tel qu'une meute ailée,
　　Le voyageur fumant.
Entre le ciel et lui, comme un tourbillon sombre,
Il les voit, puis les perd, et les entend dans l'ombre
　　Voler confusément.

Enfin, après trois jours d'une course insensée,
Après avoir franchi fleuves à l'eau glacée,
　　Steppes, forêts, déserts,
Le cheval tombe aux cris de mille oiseaux de
　　　　proie,
Et son ongle de fer sur la pierre qu'il broie
　　Eteint ses quatre éclairs.

Voilà l'infortuné, gisant, nu, misérable,
Tout tacheté de sang, plus rouge que l'érable
　　Dans la saison des fleurs.
Le nuage d'oiseaux sur lui tourne et s'arrête;
Maint bec ardent aspire à ronger dans sa tête
　　Ses yeux brûlés de pleurs!

Eh bien! ce condamné qui hurle et qui se traîne,
Ce cadavre vivant, les tribus de l'Ukraine
　　Le feront prince un jour.
Un jour, semant les champs de morts sans
　　　　sépultures,
Il dédommagera par de larges pâtures
　　L'orfraie et le vautour.

Sa sauvage grandeur naîtra de son supplice.
Un jour, des vieux hetmans il ceindra la pelisse,
　　Grand à l'œil ébloui;
Et quand il passera, ces peuples de la tente,
Prosternés, enverront la fanfare éclatante
　　Bondir autour de lui!

His eye gleams and flickers, his matted locks wander,
His head sinks: what splashes of blood are
　　　　those yonder
　　On bramble and stone?
The cords on his swollen limbs biting yet deeper,
And like a lithe serpent or venomous creeper
　　Contracting their zone.

The horse, neither bridle nor bit on him feeling,
Flies ever; red drops o'er the victim are stealing;
　　His whole body bleeds.
Alas! to the wild horses foaming and champing,
That followed with manes erect, neighing and
　　　　stamping,
　　A crow-flight succeeds.

The raven, the horn'd owl with eyes round and
　　　　hollow,
The osprey and eagle from battle-field follow,
　　Though daylight alarm.
The carrion crow and the vulture so bloody,
Which plunges 'mid corpses its neck bare and
　　　　ruddy,
　　Just like a bare arm.

All hasten to swell the procession so dreary,
And many a league from the holm or the eyrie
　　They follow this man.
Mazeppa, scarce hearing what sound the air sunders,
Looks up; who can that be unfolding, he wonders,
　　A mighty black fan?

The gloomy night falls with no stars penetrating;
More keen is the chase in impatience awaiting
　　Until his breath quit;
As a strange and mysterious whirlwind he fears
　　　　them,
They flash and are gone, then in darkness he
　　　　hears them
　　Confusedly flit.

Then after three days of this course wild and
　　　　frantic,
Through rivers of ice, plains and forests gigantic,
　　The horse sinks and dies;
His limbs quiver faintly, his struggles are over,
And once more the birds of prey circle and hover
　　Where low the prince lies.

Behold him there naked, blood-stained and
　　　　despairing,
All red, like the foliage of autumn preparing
　　To wither and fall.
The birds hanging o'er him now soaring like rockets,
Now dropping again to tear out of their sockets
　　Each tear-smarting ball.

Yet mark! That poor sufferer, gasping and
　　　　moaning,
To-morrow the Cossacks of Ukraine atoning,
　　Will hail as their king;
And soon in his might, o'er the battle-tide rolling,
His thousands he'll sway, and a harvest consoling
　　To vultures will fling.

No more in obscurity destined to languish,
The rule of a kingdom will solace his anguish
　　A crown on his brow:
To royal Mazeppa the hordes Asiatic
Will shout their devotion in fervour ecstatic,
　　And low to earth bow.

II

So, wenn ein Sterblicher, den Gott empfunden
Tief in der Brust, und fühlet sich gebunden
  An den Geist, der ihn trägt.
O Genius, feurig Ross! umsonst sein Ringen,
Des Lebens Schranken wirst du überspringen,
  Die dein Huftritt zerschlägt.

Du führst durch Wüsten ihn, auf eis'ge Gipfel,
Durch Meeresflut und über moos'ge Wipfel
  Zu den Wolken empor,
Und Nachtgestalten, die du aufgescheuchet,
Umdrängen ihn, es krächzt um ihn und keuchet,
  Der gespenstische Chor.

Du lässest ihn auf deinen Feuerschwingen
Die Körperwelt, die Geisterwelt durchdringen,
  An dem ewigen Strom
Tränkest du ihn, und wo Kometen streifen,
Lässt du sein Haupthaar unter Sternen schweifen
  Hoch am himmlischen Dom.

Die Monde Herschels und mit seinen Ringen
Saturn, den Pol, um dessen Stirn sich schlingen
  Diademe von Licht,
Er sieht sie all', auf schrankenlosem Gleise
Erweiterst unaufhörlich du die Kreise
  Seinem geist'gen Gesicht.

Nur Engel und Dämone mögen ahnen,
Welch' Leiden ihn auf nie betretnen Bahnen

  Ueberwältigen mag,
Wenn Flammen er in tiefster Seele spüret,
Und ach! des Nachts, wenn ihm die Stirn be-
          rührt
  Feuchter Fittiche Schlag.

Er stöhnt entsetzt — du reissest unaufhaltsam
Den Schreckensbleichen fort im Flug gewaltsam,
  Dass er zittert und bebt,
Bei jedem Schritt scheint er dem Tod zum Raube,
Bis er sich neigt und stürzt, und aus dem Staube
  Sich ein König erhebt.
                    V. Hugo.
              (Übers. v. P. Cornelius.)

Ainsi, lorsqu'un mortel, sur qui son dieu s'étale,
S'est vu lié vivant sur ta croupe fatale,
  Génie, ardent coursier,
En vain il lutte, hélas! tu bondis, tu l'emportes
Hors du monde réel dont tu brises les portes
  Avec tes pieds d'acier!

Tu franchis avec lui déserts, cimes chenues
Des vieux monts, et les mers, et, par delà les nues,
  De sombres régions;
Et mille impurs esprits que ta course réveille
Autour du voyageur, insolente merveille,
  Pressent leurs légions!

Il traverse d'un vol, sur tes ailes de flamme,
Tous les champs du possible, et les mondes de
          l'âme;
  Boit au fleuve éternel;
Dans la nuit orageuse ou la nuit étoilée,
Sa chevelure, aux crins des comètes mêlée,
  Flamboie au front du ciel.

Les six lunes d'Herschel, l'anneau du vieux
          Saturne,
Le pôle, arrondissant une aurore nocturne
  Sur son front boréal.
Il voit tout; et pour lui ton vol, que rien ne
          lasse,
De ce monde sans borne à chaque instant déplace
  L'horizon idéal.

Qui peut savoir, hormis les démons et les anges,
Ce qu'il souffre, à te suivre et quels éclairs
          étranges
      A ses yeux reluiront,
Comme il sera brûlé d'ardentes étincelles,
Hélas! et dans la nuit combien de froides ailes
  Viendront battre son front!

Il crie épouvanté, tu poursuis implacable.
Pâle, épuisé, béant, sous ton vol qui l'accable
  Il ploie avec effroi;
Chaque pas que tu fais semble creuser sa tombe.
Enfin le terme arrive . . . il court, il vole, il
          tombe,
      Et se relève roi!
              V. Hugo.

So when a poor mortal whose brains the gods addle
O Pegasus! finds himself bound to thy saddle,
  His fate is as meet.
Away from the world — from all real existence,
Thou bearest him upward, despite his resistance,
  On metrical feet!

Thou tak'st him o'er deserts, o'er mountains in
          legions,
Grey-hoary, thro' oceans and into the regions
  Right up in the clouds;
A thousand base spirits his progress unshaken
Arouses, press round him and stare as they waken,
  In insolent crowds.

He traverses, soaring on fiery pinions,
All fields of creation, all spirit dominions
  And drains Heaven dry:
Thro' darkness and storm, or 'mid stars brightly
          gleaming,
See Pegasus' tail like a comet is streaming
  Across the whole sky.

The six moons of Herschel, the ringéd horizon
Of Saturn, the pole whose white forehead bedizen
  The weird Northern lights,
All views he: for him in this flight never ending
The infinite bounds of his vision extending,
  Yield fresh Pisgah sights.

Who can know, save the angels amid whom he
          dashes,
What anguish he suffers and what mystic flashes
  Illumine his sight?
What fiery darts lend his spirit their fuel,
And ah! what nocturnal wings icy and cruel
  Extinguish the light?

He cries out with terror, in agony gasping,
Yet ever the neck of his hippogrif clasping,
  They heavenward spring;
Each leap that he takes with fresh woe is attended:
He totters — falls lifeless — the struggle is
          ended —
    We hail him then king!   V. Hugo.
              (Translated by F. Corder.)

INSTRUMENTATION

2 Flutes

Piccolo

2 Oboes

English Horn

2 Clarinets

Bass Clarinet

2 Bassoons

4 Horns

3 Trumpets

3 Trombones

Tuba

Timpani

Percussion

(Triangle Bass Drum, Cymbals)

Violins I

Violins II

Violas

Violoncellos

Basses

Duration: ca. 18 minutes

First Performance: April 16, 1854
Weimar: Hofkapelle
Franz Liszt, conductor

ISBN: 978-1-60874-026-0

This score is an unabridged reprint of the score
first issued in Leipzig by Breitkopf & Härtel, 1909. Plate F.L. 6

Printed in the USA
First Printing: December, 2011

MAZEPPA
Symphonic Poem No. 6
S. 100

FRANZ LISZT (1811-1886)

*) Der Schlusssatz (von Seite 73 Allegro ₵ an beginnend) kann ohne das Vorhergehende separat aufgeführt werden. (Spätere Anmerkung von Fr. Liszt.)
The final part (commencing at page 73, Allegro ₵) can be performed separately, without the opening portion. (Later remark by Fr. Liszt.)
On peut faire exécuter à part la partie finale (en commençant à la page 73, Allegro ₵) sans la partie precédente. (Note tardive de Fr. Liszt.)

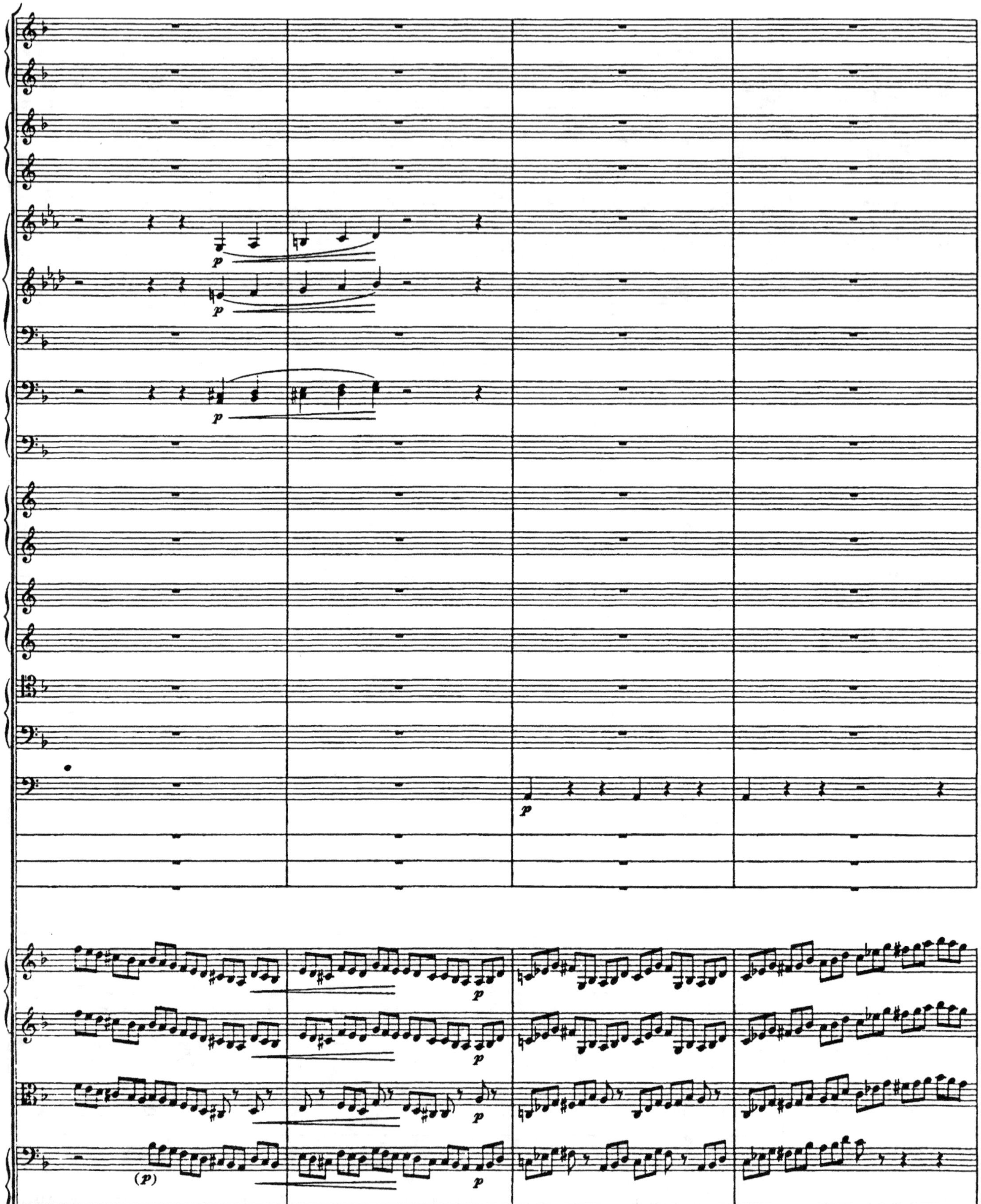
p
(p)

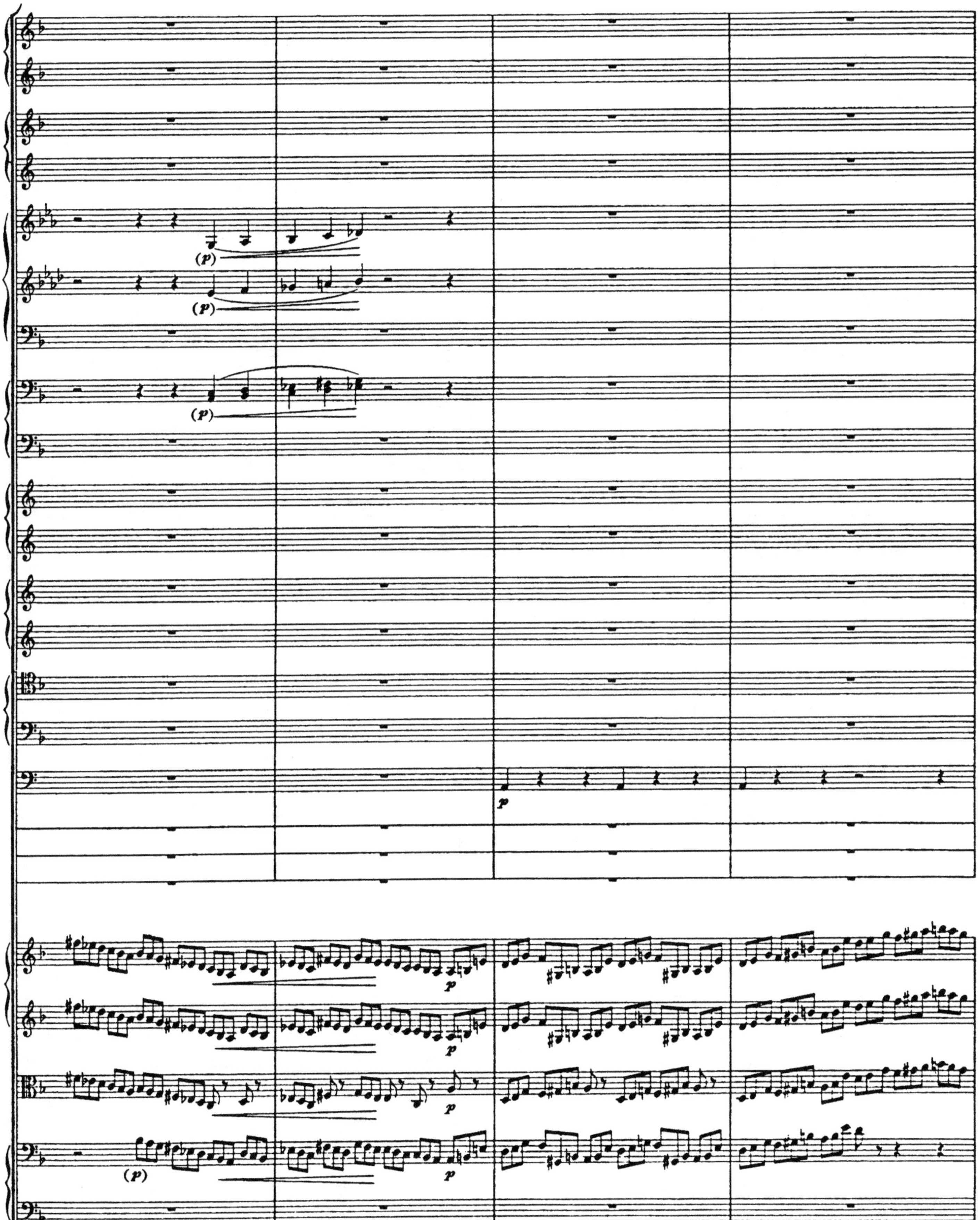
(p)
(p)
(p)
p
p
p
p
(p)
p

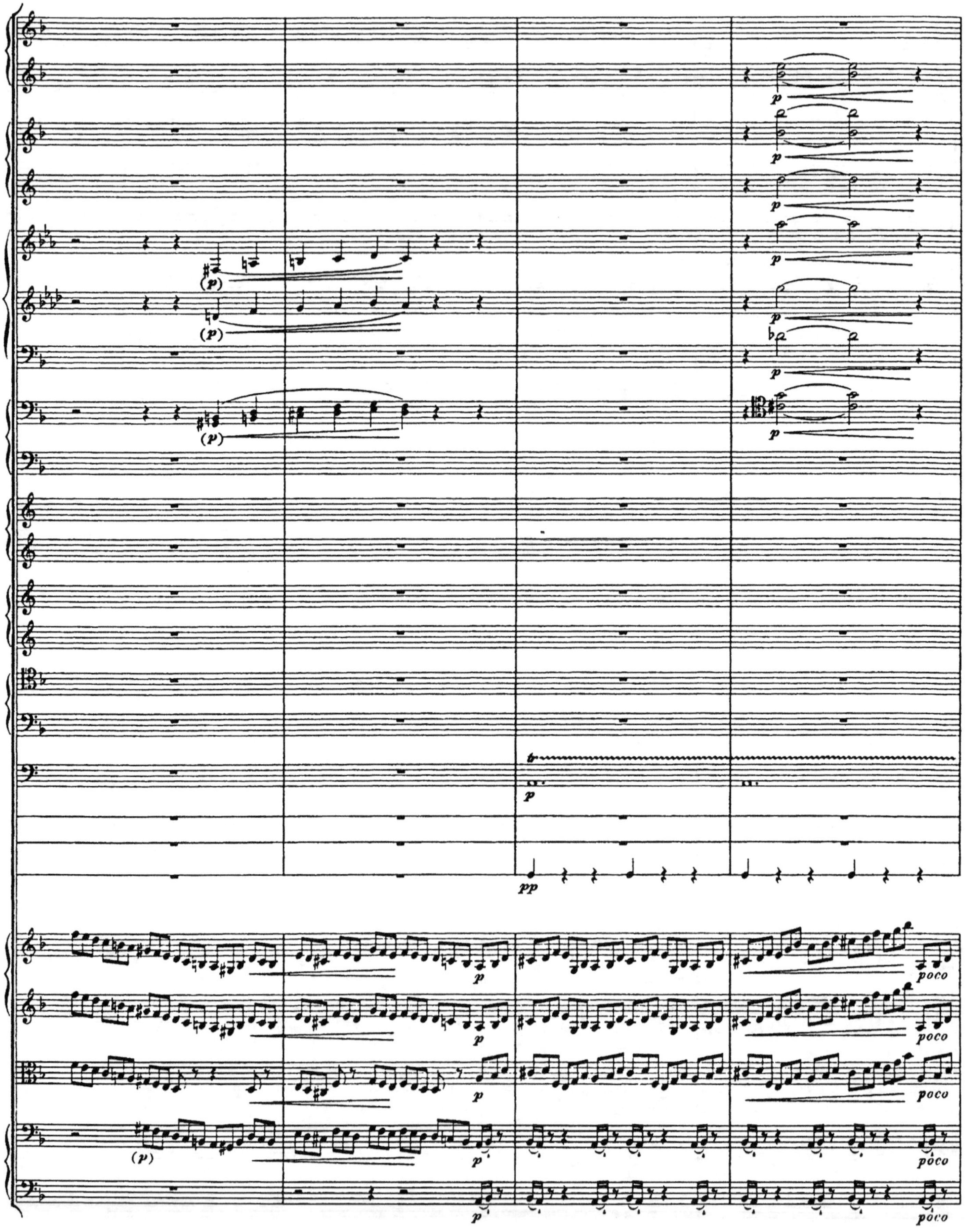
poco

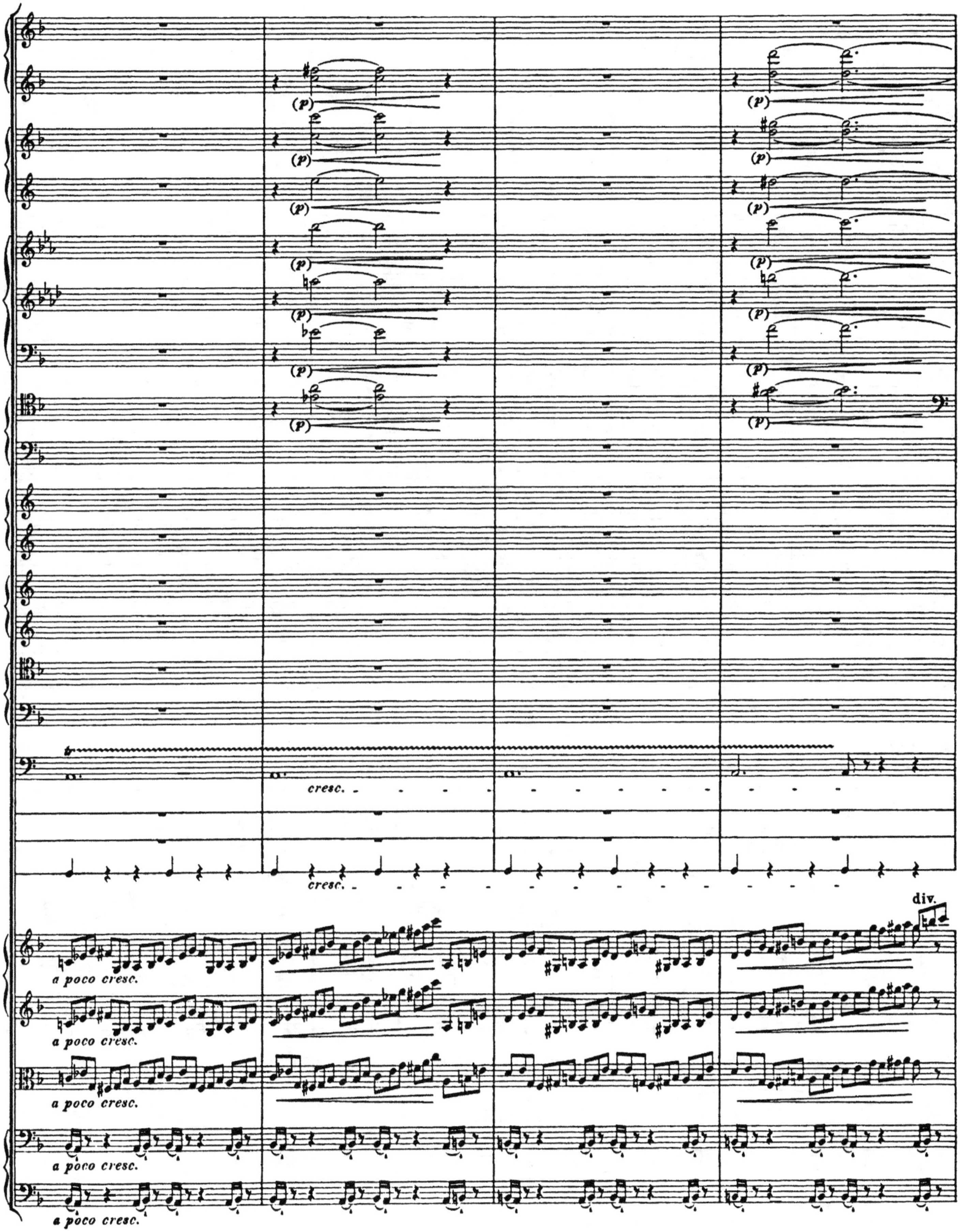

a 2.
più cresc.
più cresc.
più cresc.
più cresc.
più cresc.
più cresc.
più cresc.

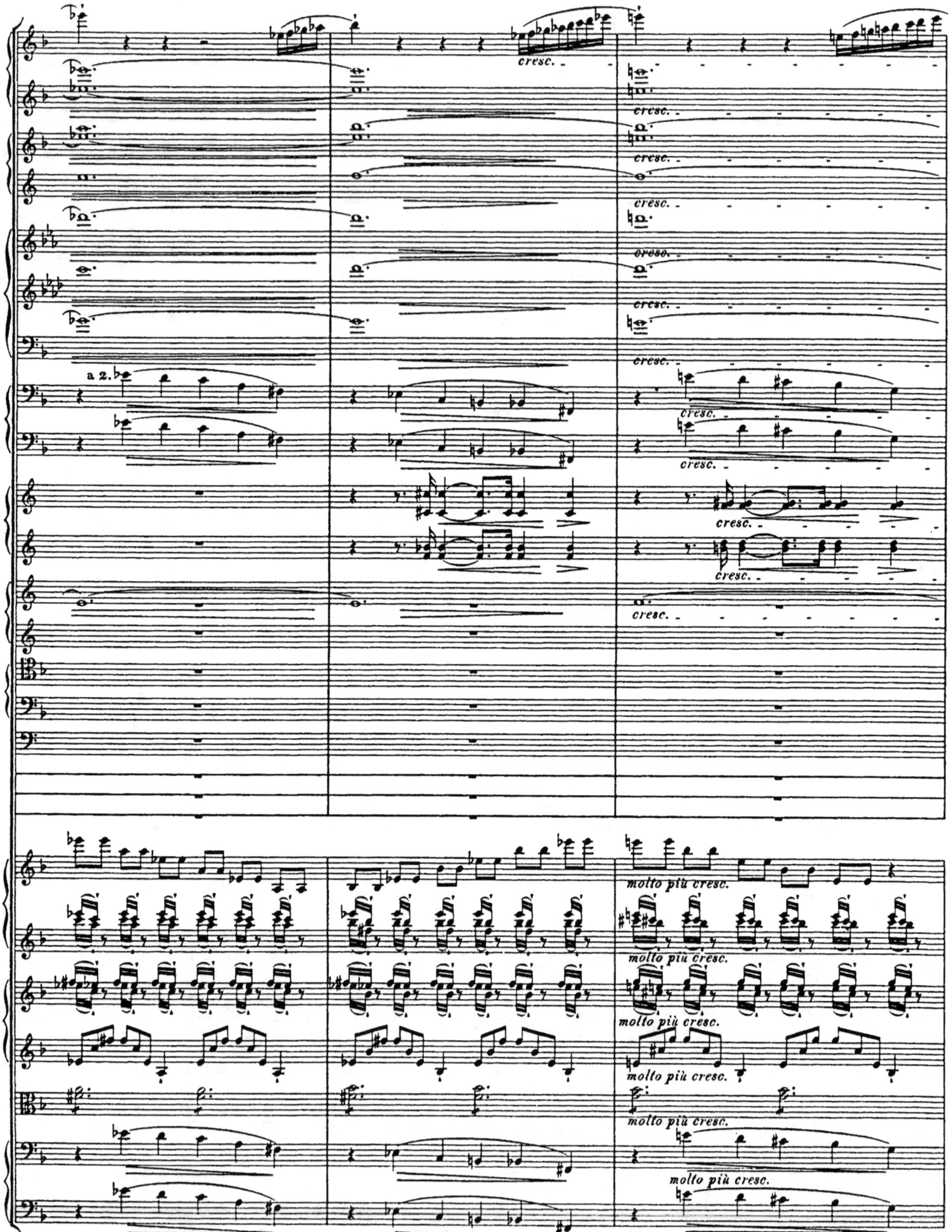
cresc.
a 2.
molto più cresc.

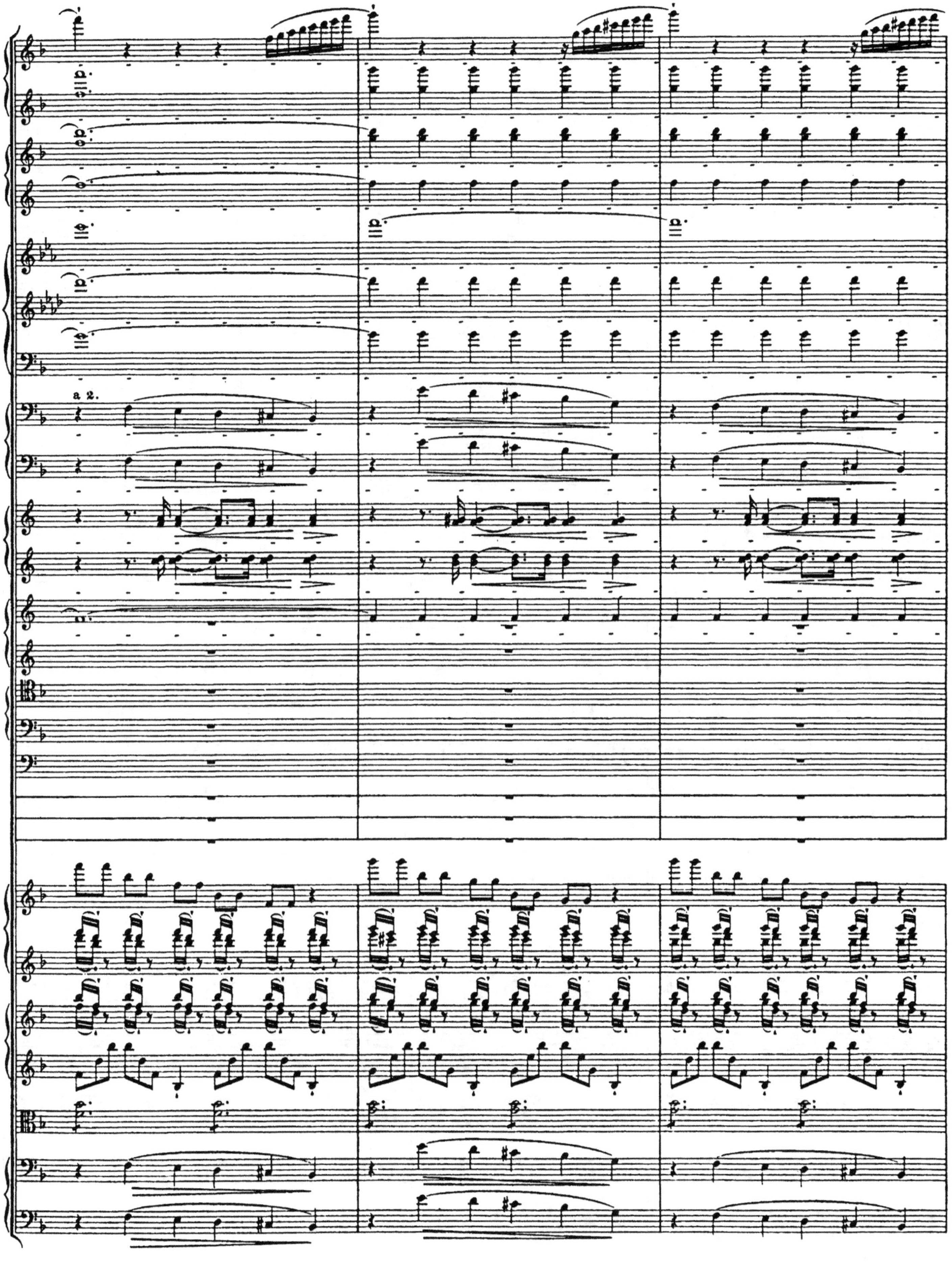
a 2.

a 2.
a 2.
unis.
unis.
stringendo
stringendo
stringendo
stringendo

B
a 2.
ff (sempre)
ff (sempre)
a 2.
ff (sempre)
a 2.
ff (sempre)
a 2.
ff (sempre)
a 2.
ff (sempre)
ff (sempre)
ff sempre
ff sempre
ff sempre
ff sempre
ff sempre
B

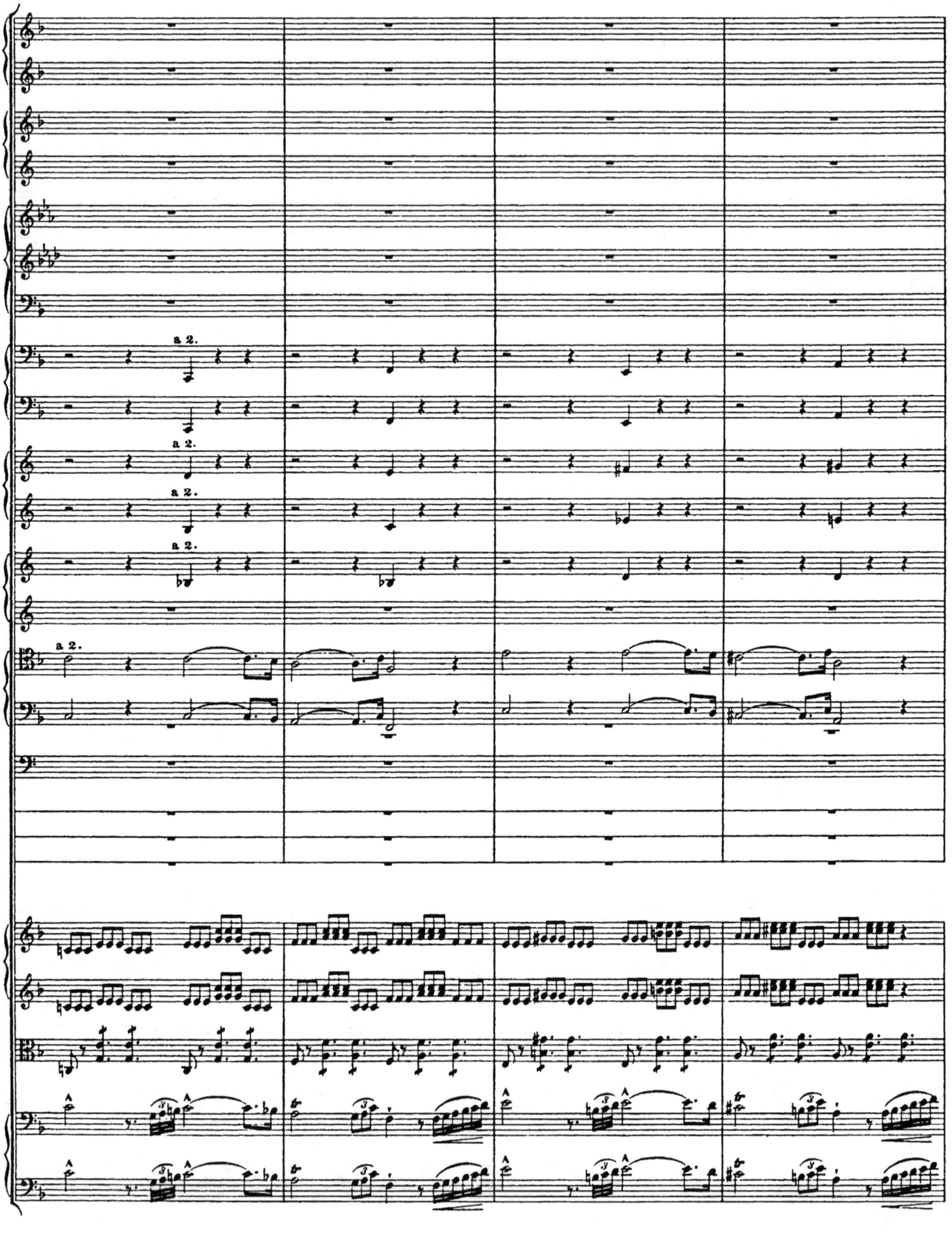
a 2.
a 2.
a 2.
a 2.
a 2.

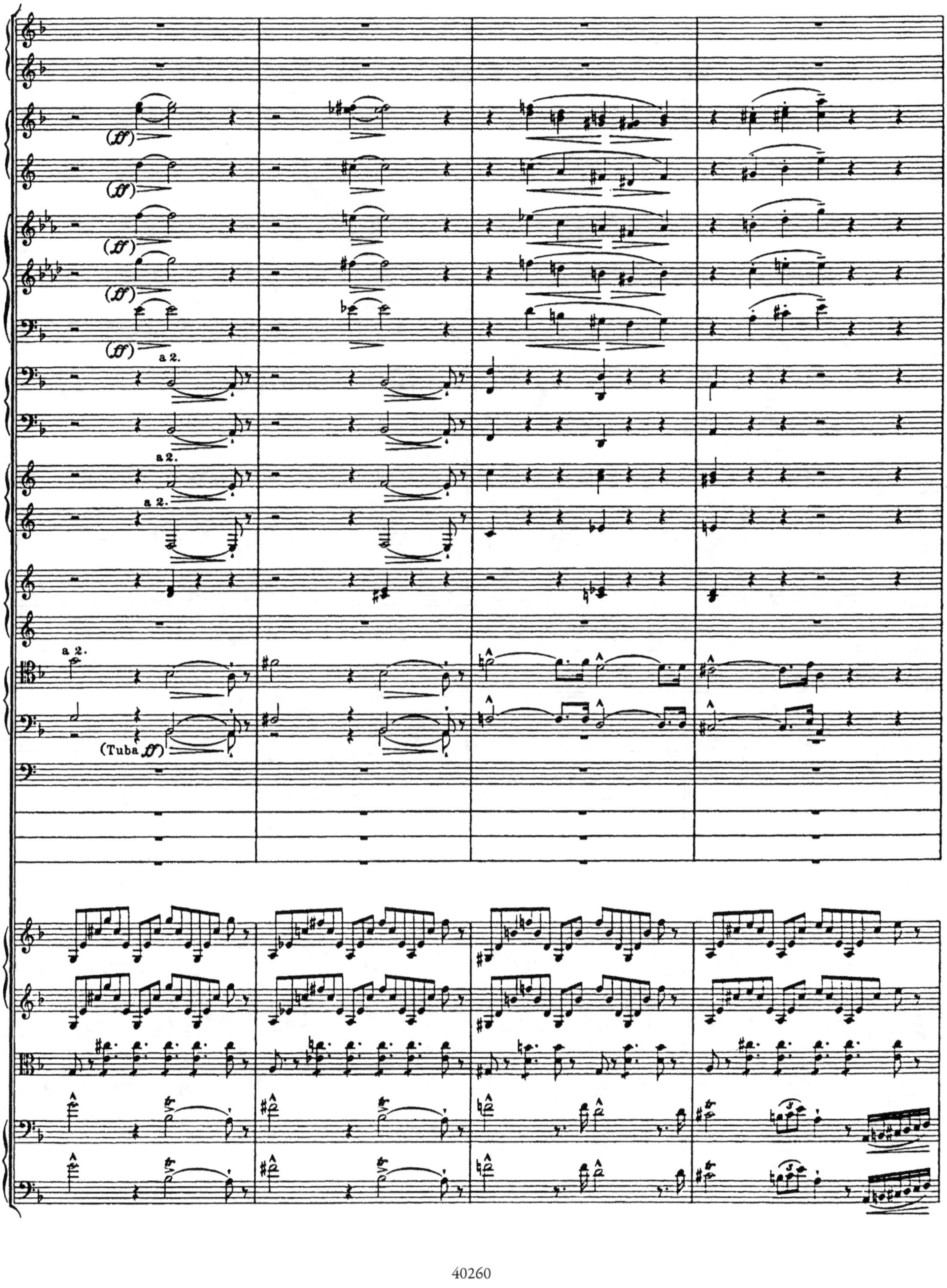
(ff)
a 2.
(Tuba ff)

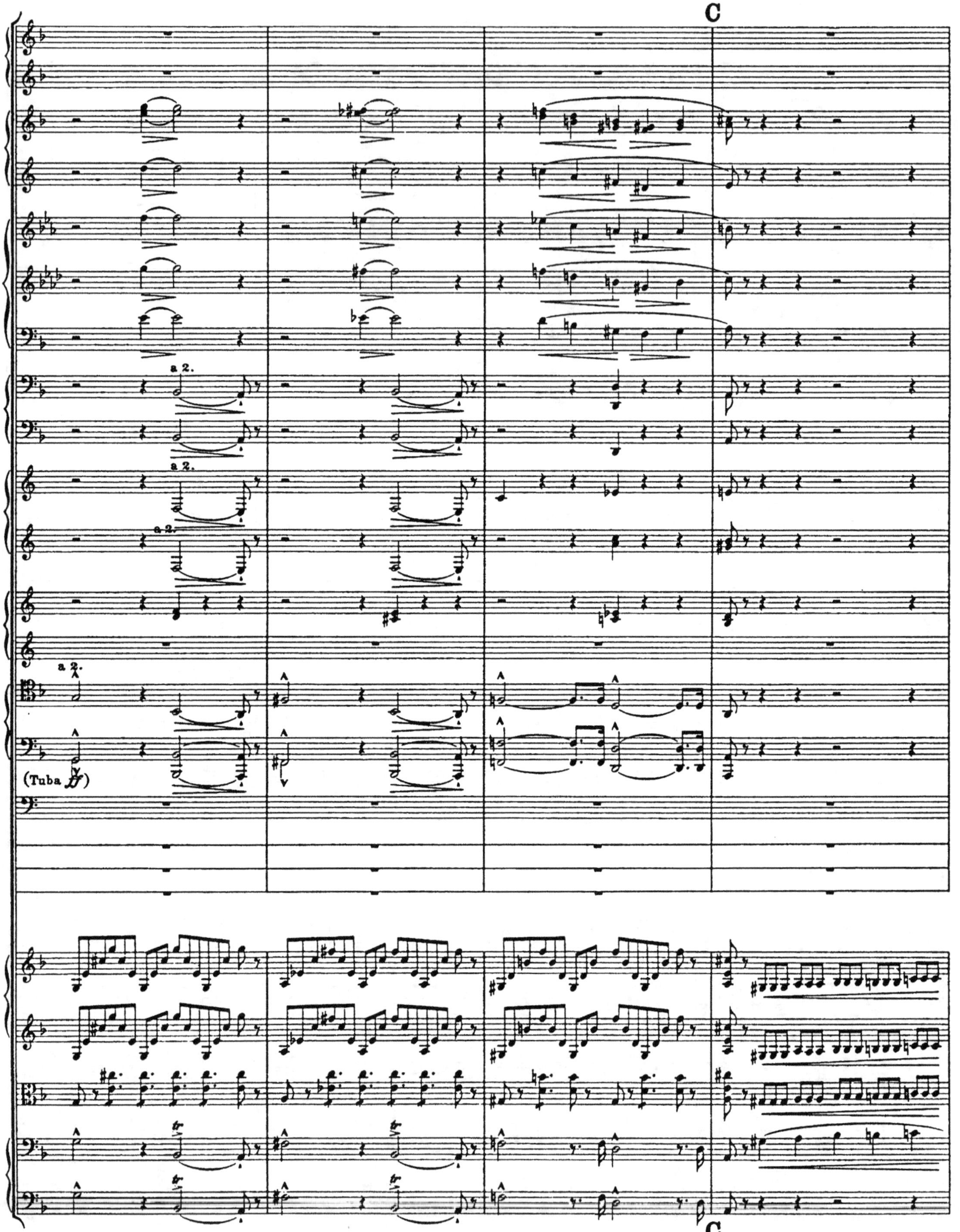
C
a 2.
a 2.
a 2.
a 2.
(Tuba ff)
tr
C

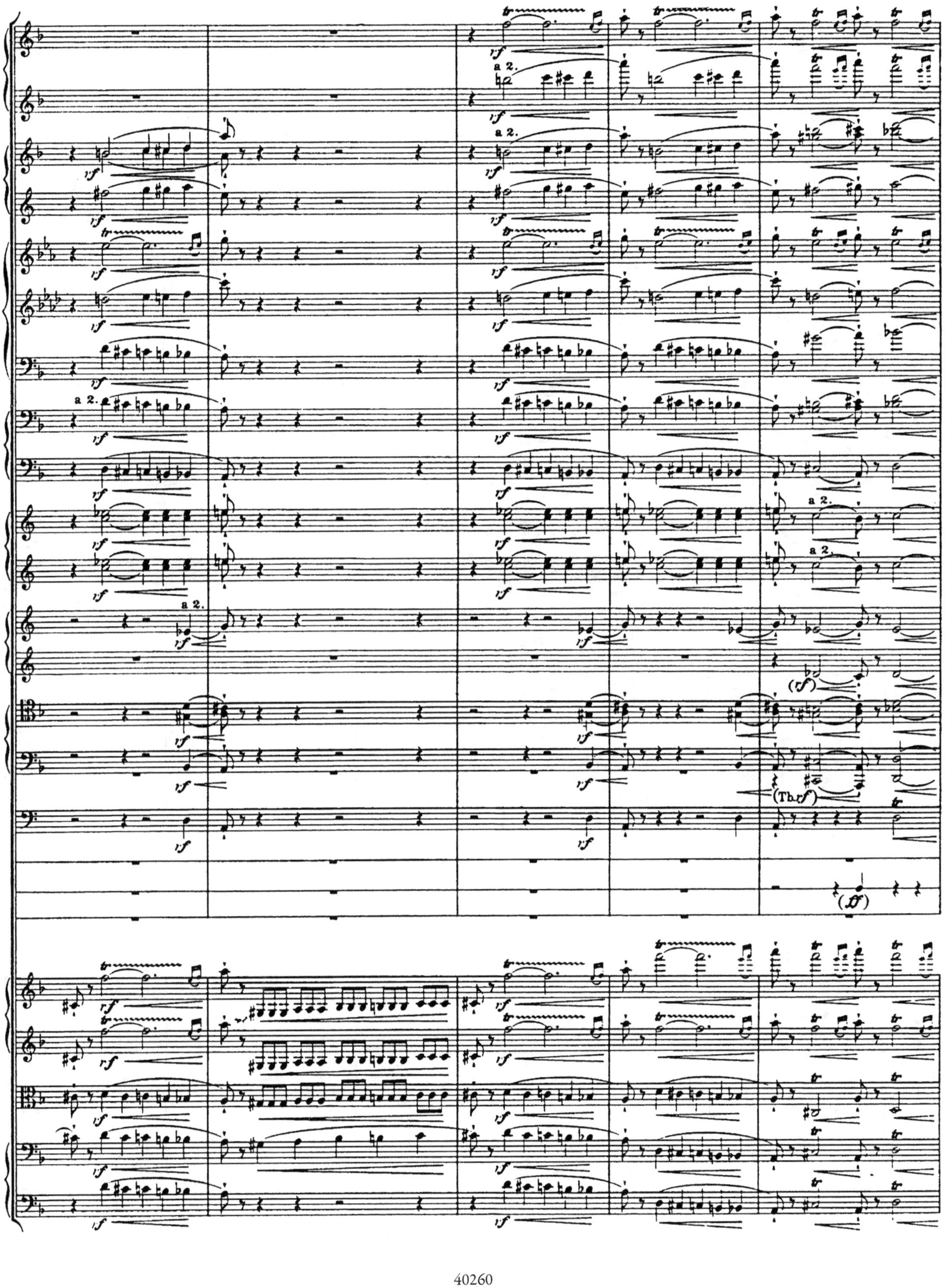
a 2.
rf
(rf)
(Thrf)
(ff)

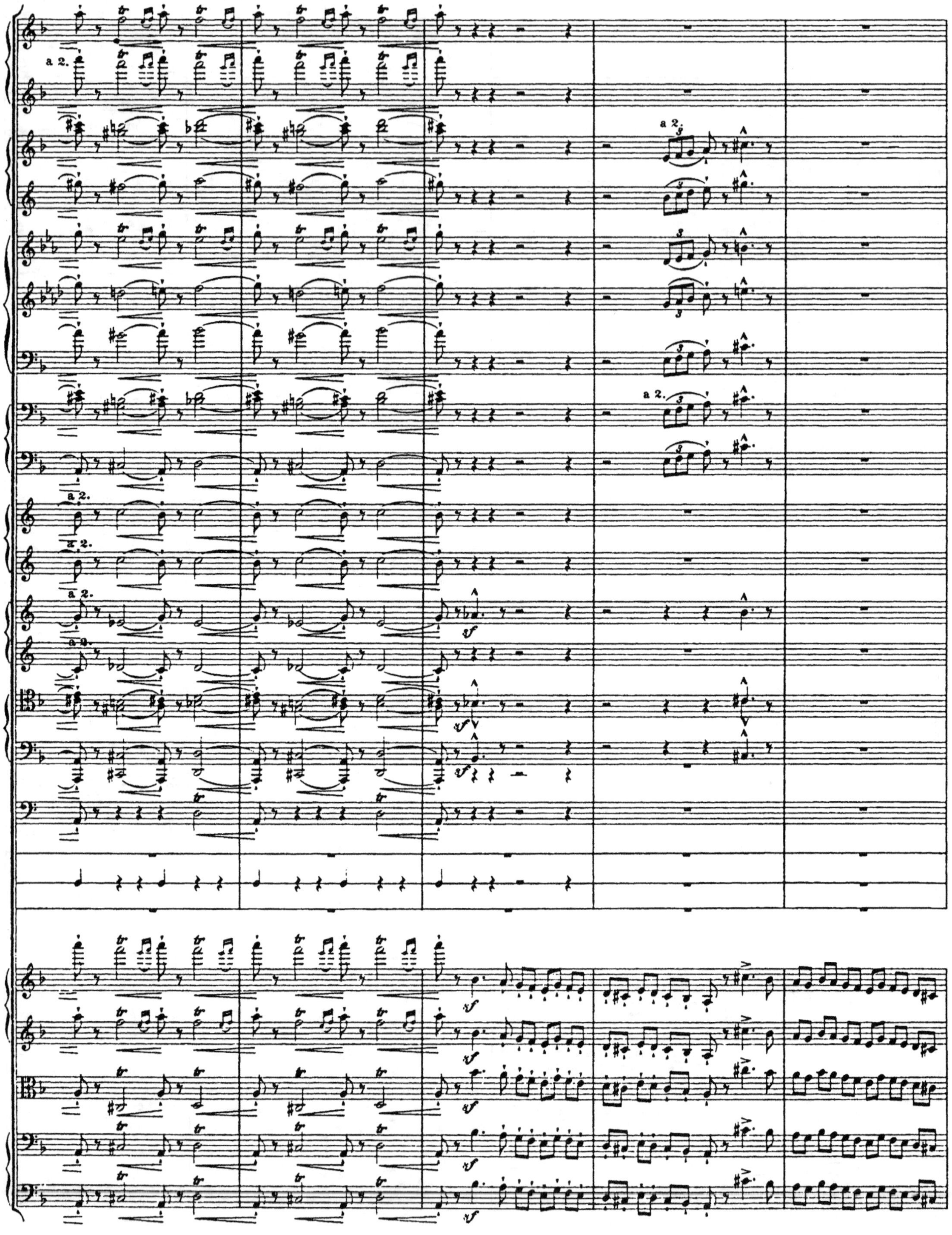
a 2.
tr
a 2.
a 2.
a 2.
a 2.
a 2.
a 2.
sf

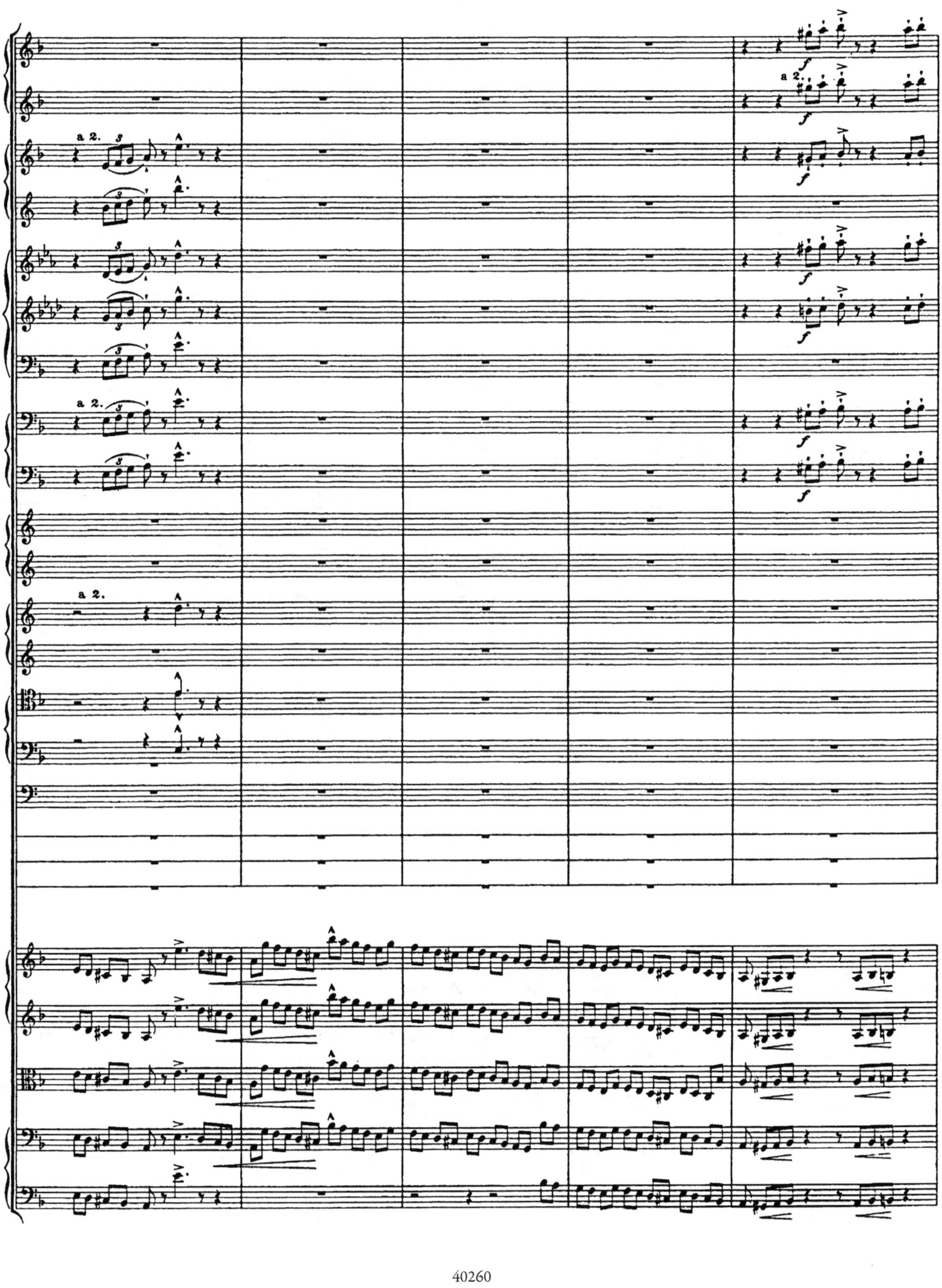
a 2.
f
a 2.
a 2.
a 2.

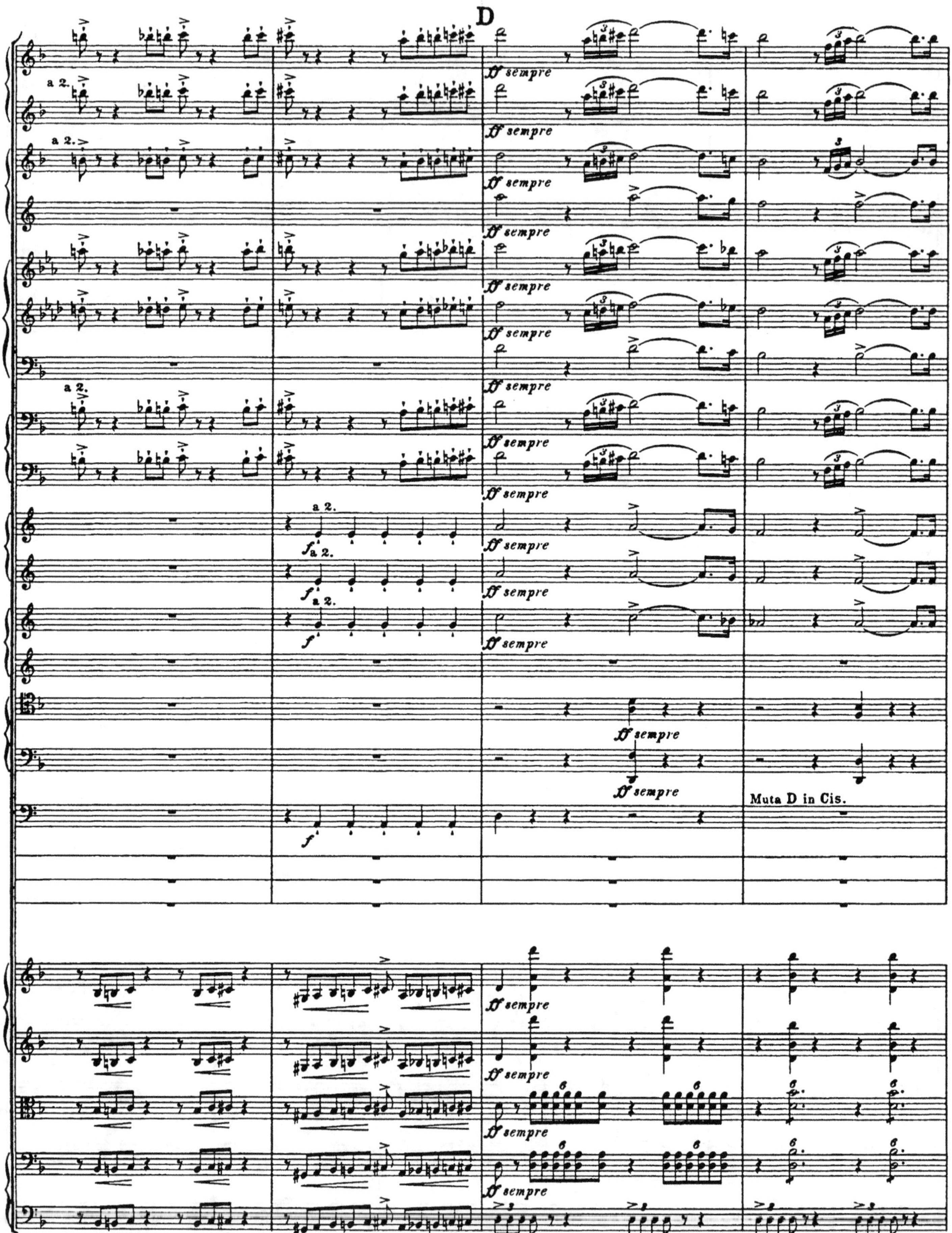
D
a 2.
ff sempre
f
Muta D in Cis.
D

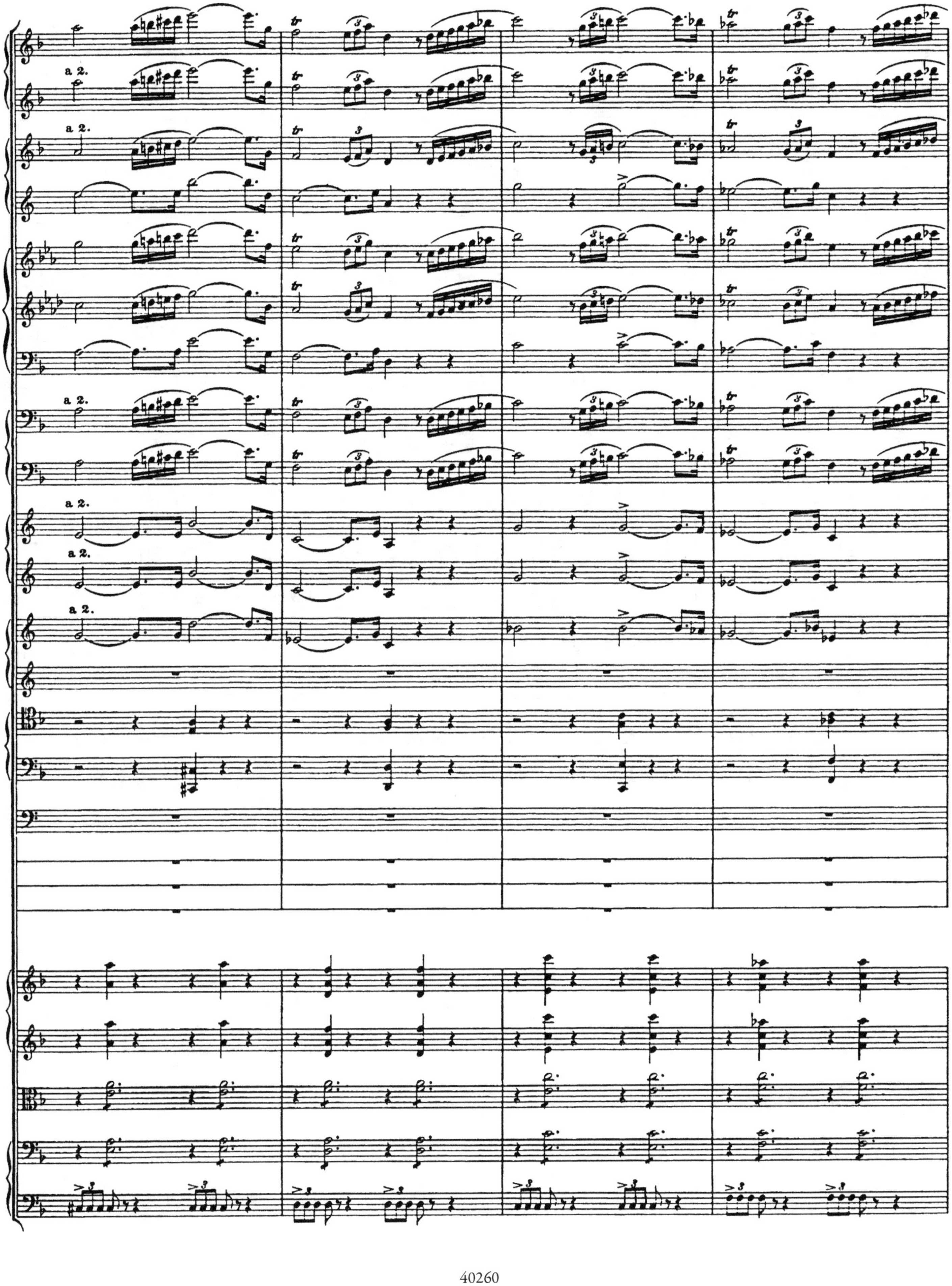
a 2.
a 2.
a 2.
a 2.
a 2.
a 2.
tr

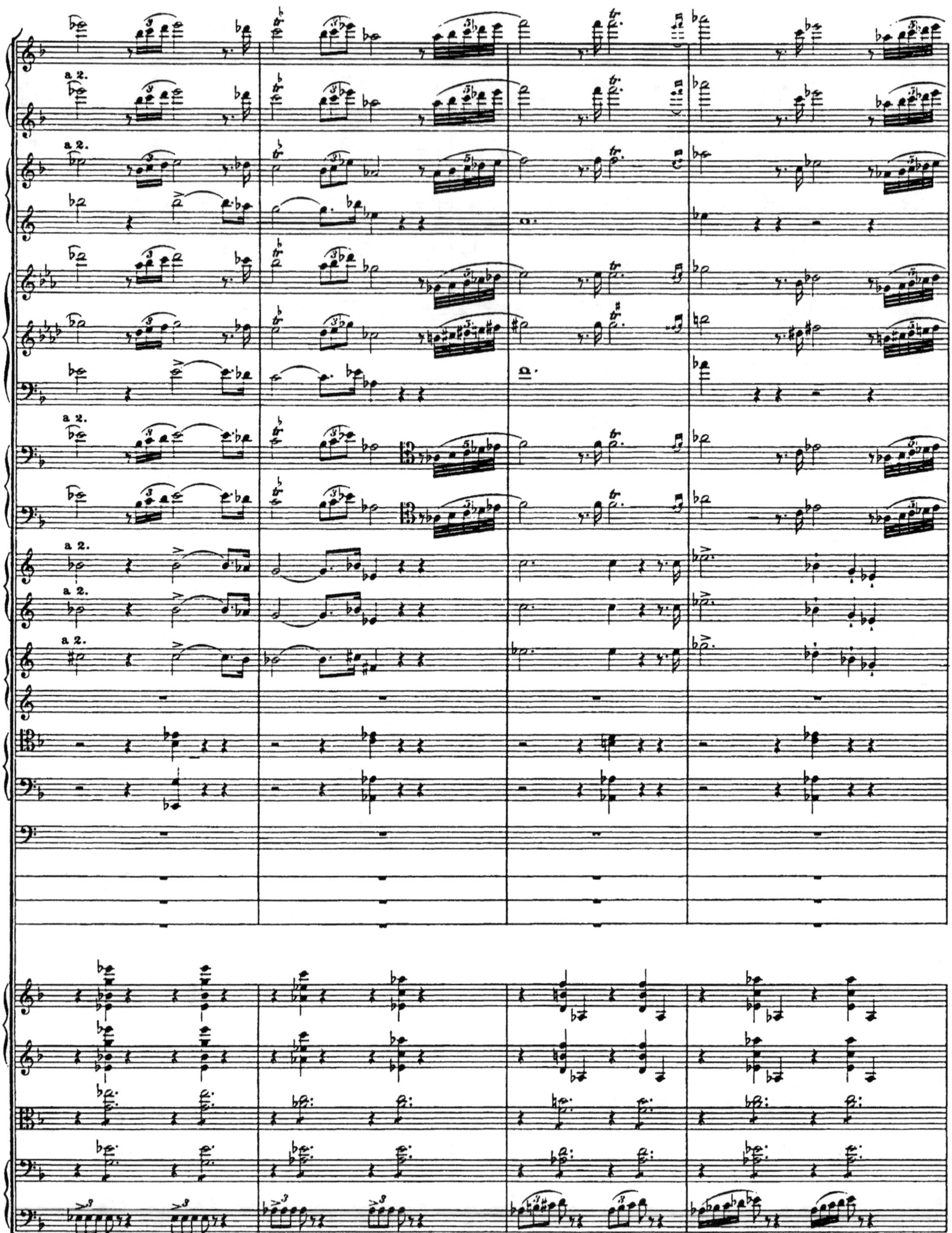
a 2.
a 2.
a 2.
a 2.
a 2.
a 2.

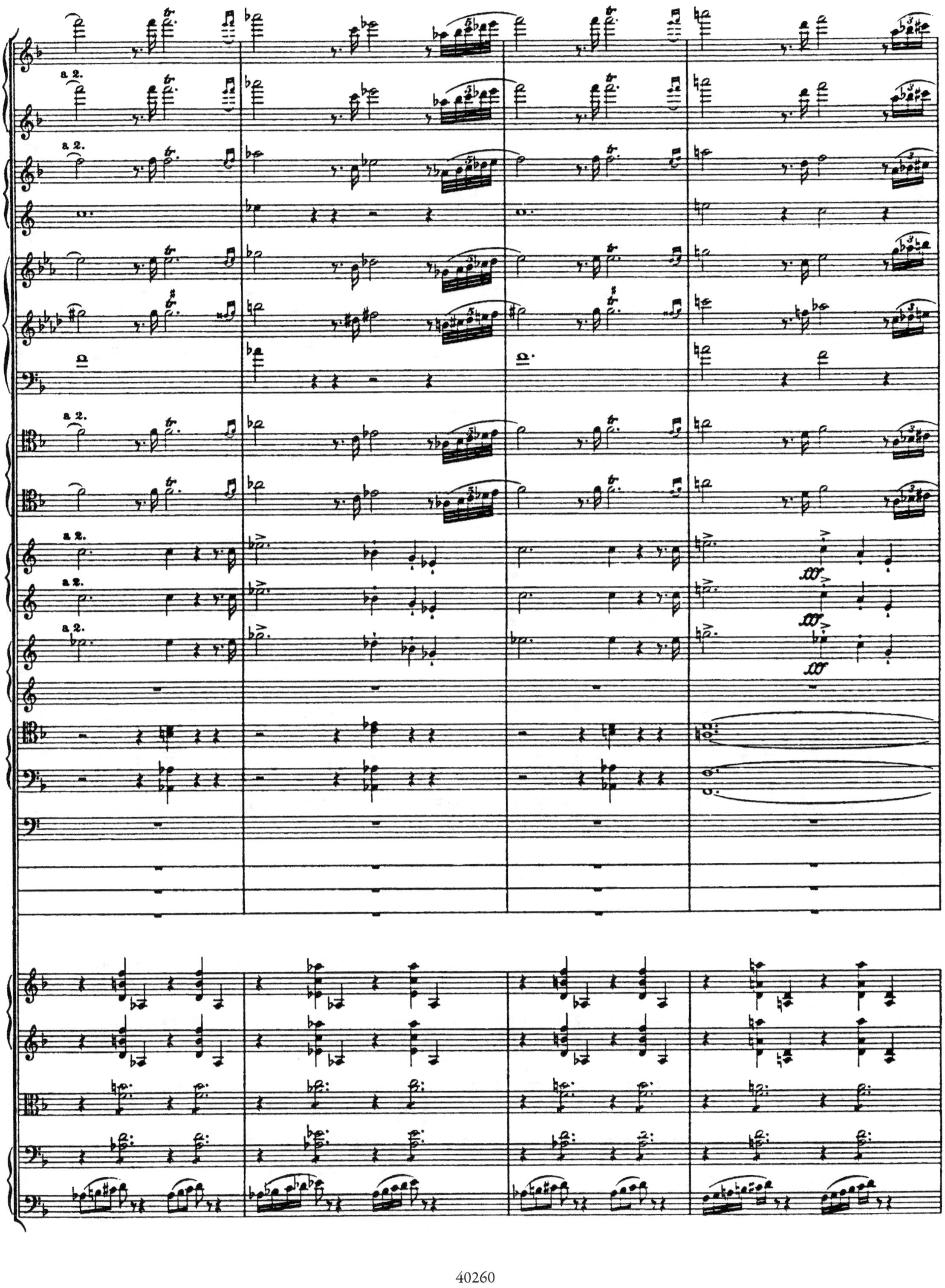
a 2.
a 2.
a 2.
a 2.
a 2.
a 2.
tr
fff

in Cis. A.

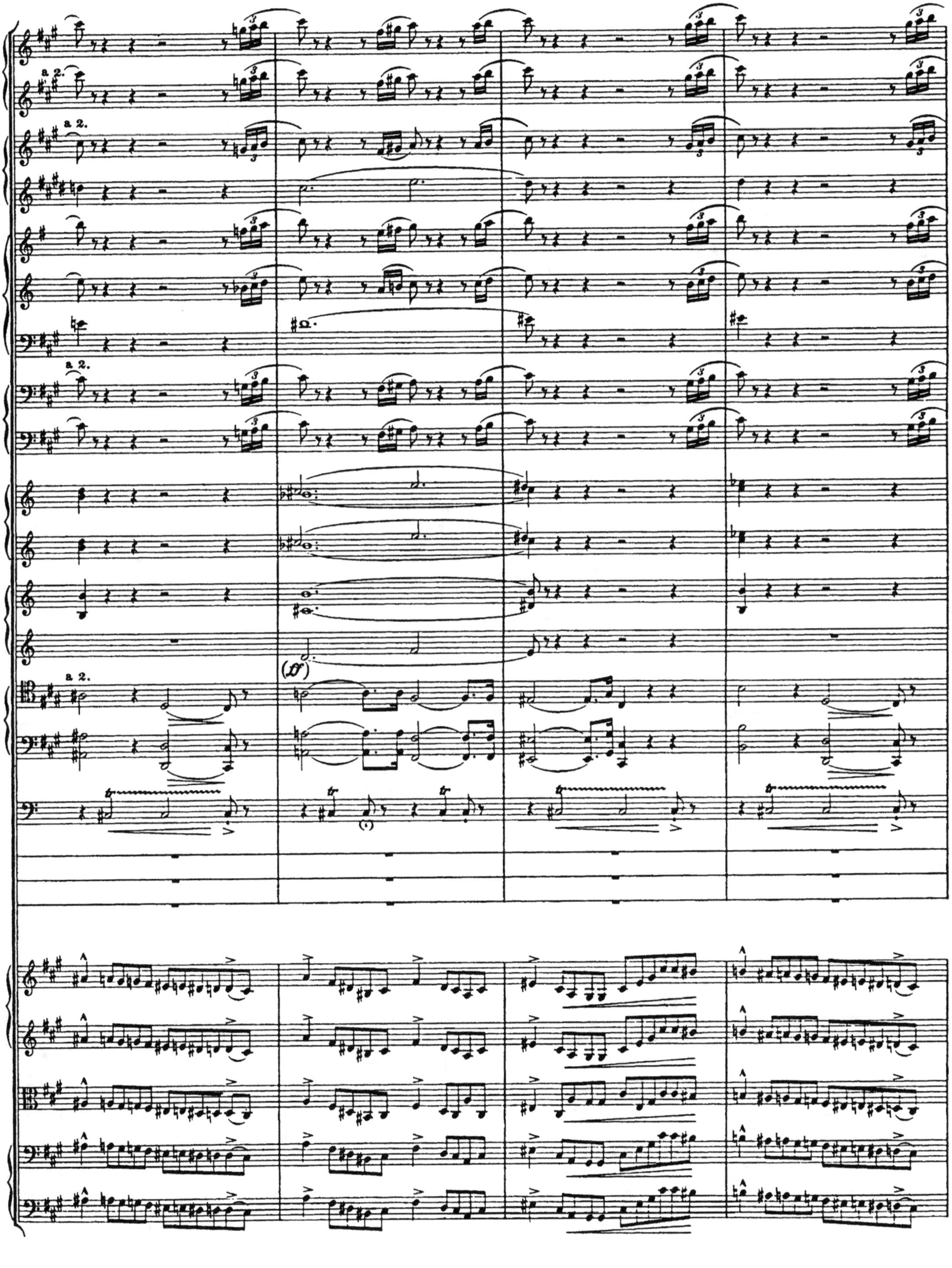
a 2.
a 2.
a 2.
(ff)
a 2.
tr

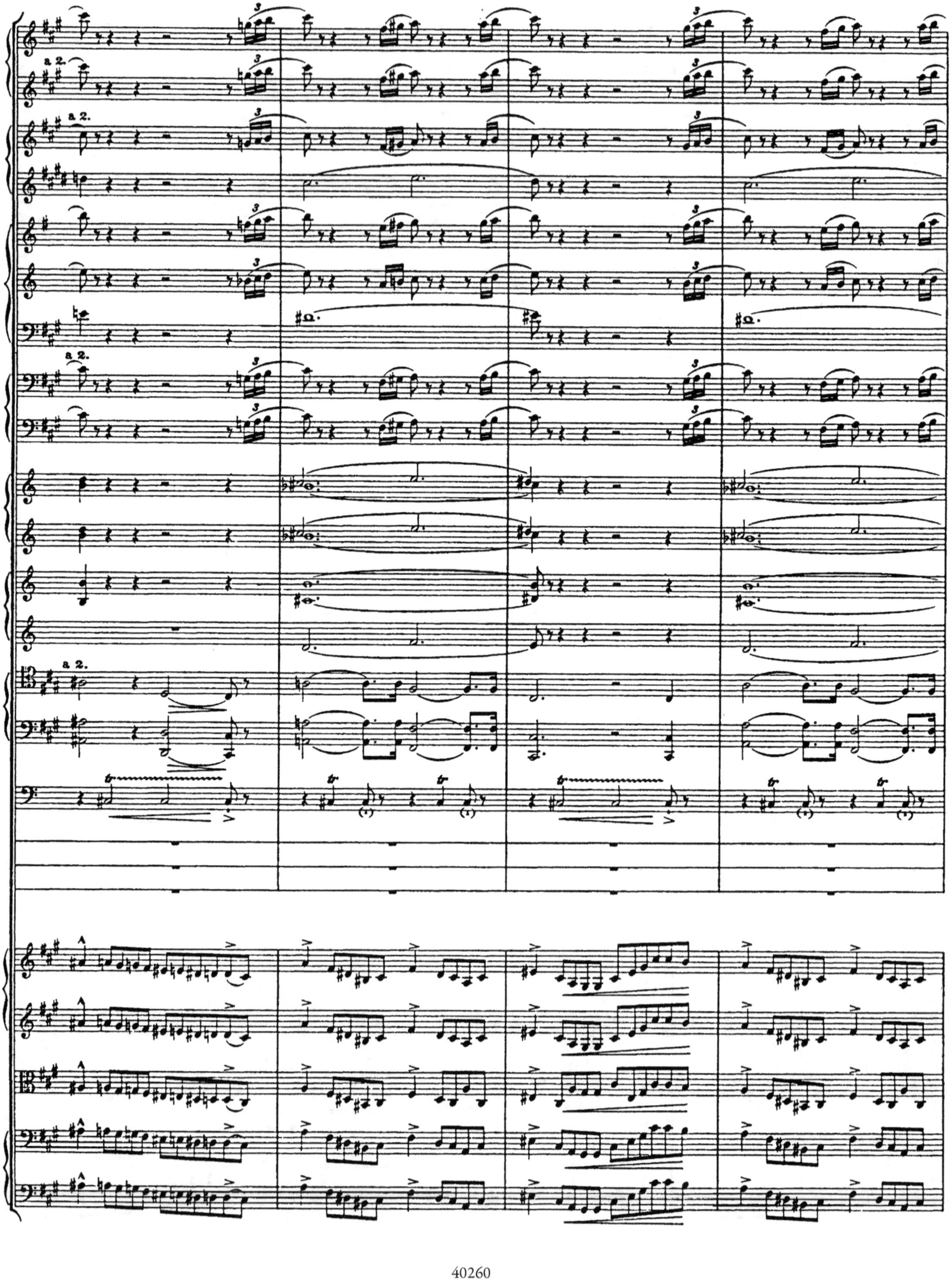
a 2.
a 2.
a 2.
a 2.
tr

Muta in Es.

Muta in D.

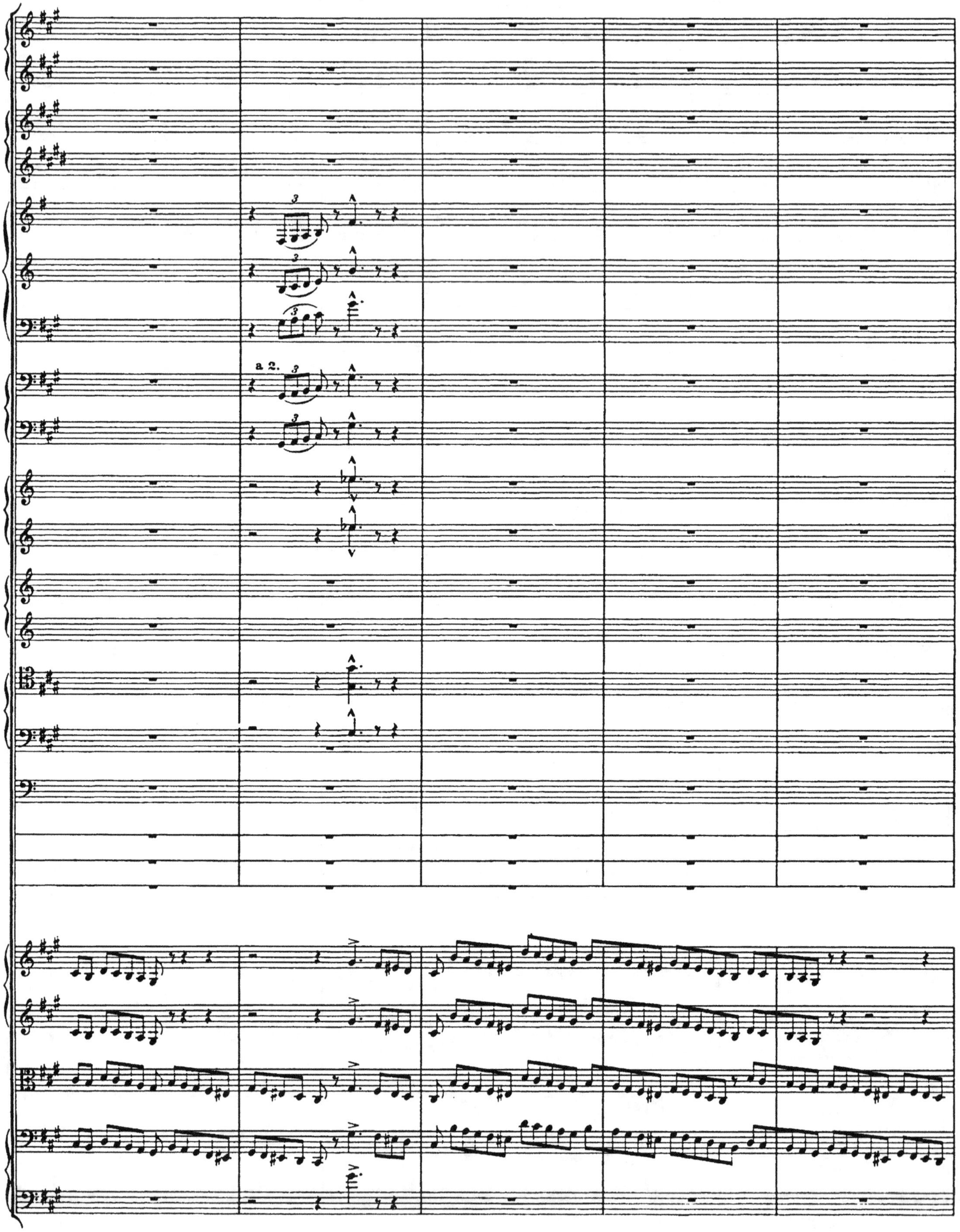
a 2.

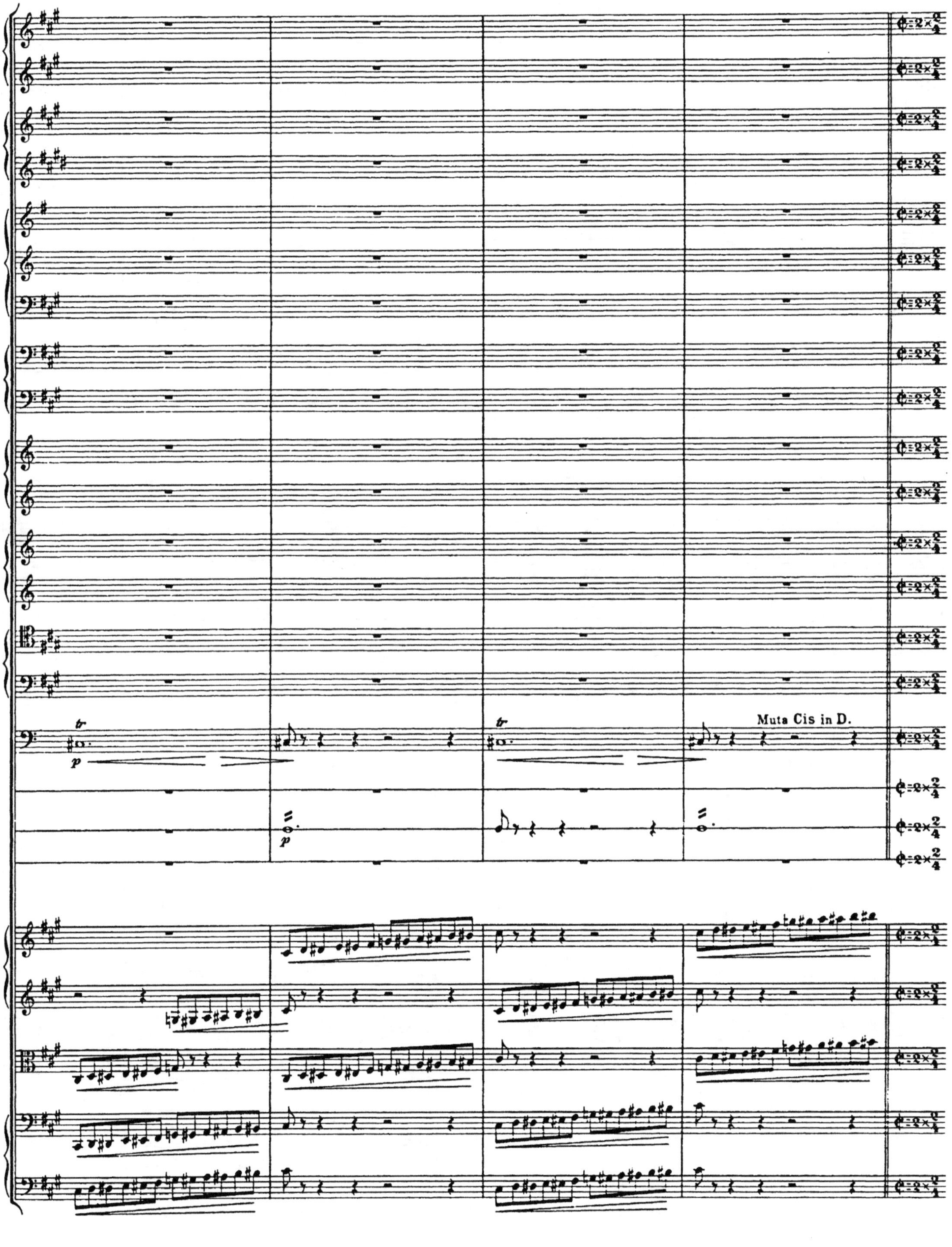
tr
p
tr
Muta Cis in D.
p

Un poco più mosso,–sempre agitato assai.

Un poco più mosso,–sempre agitato assai.

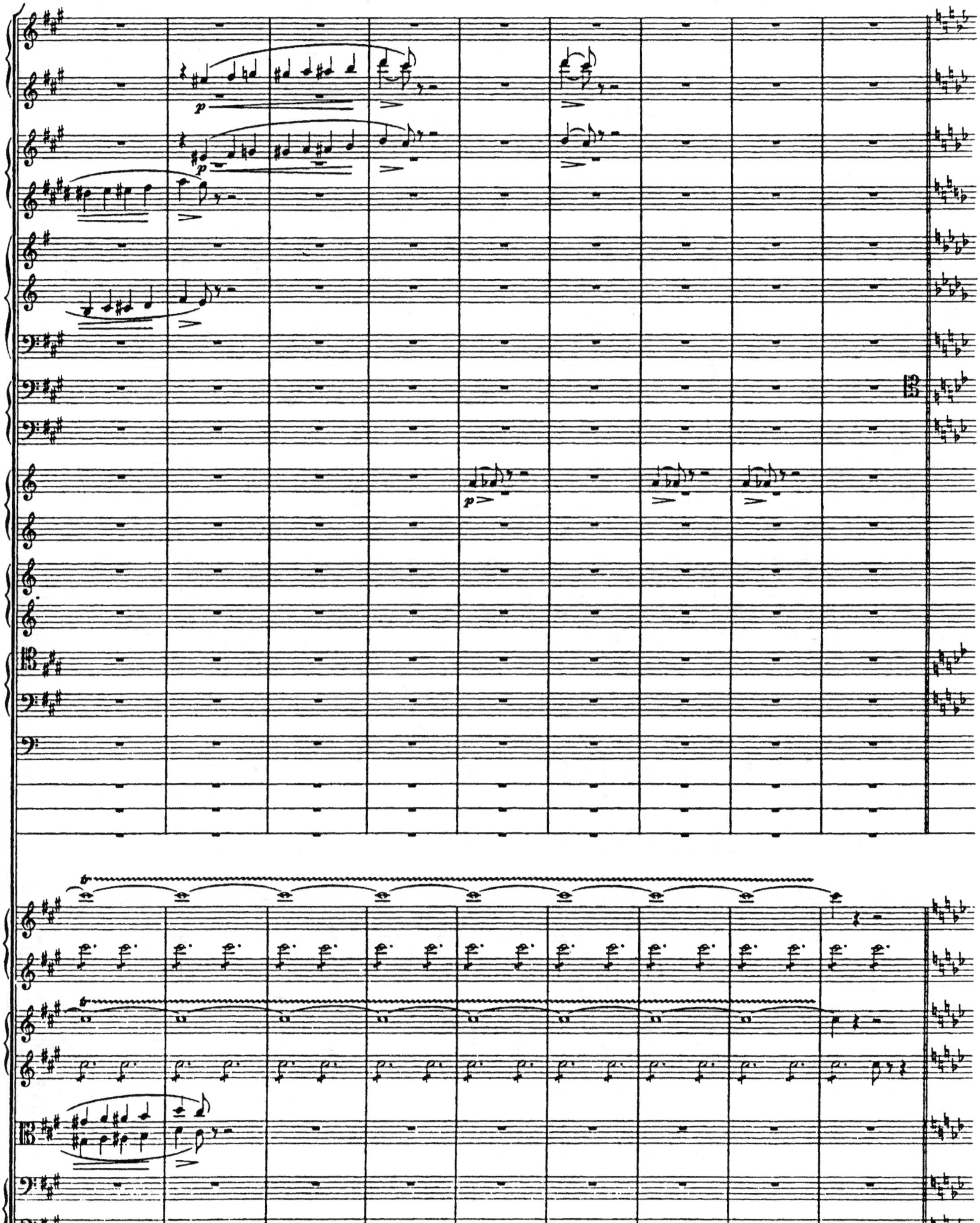

*) Zwei einzelne Violinen.
Two violins soli.
Deux violons seuls.

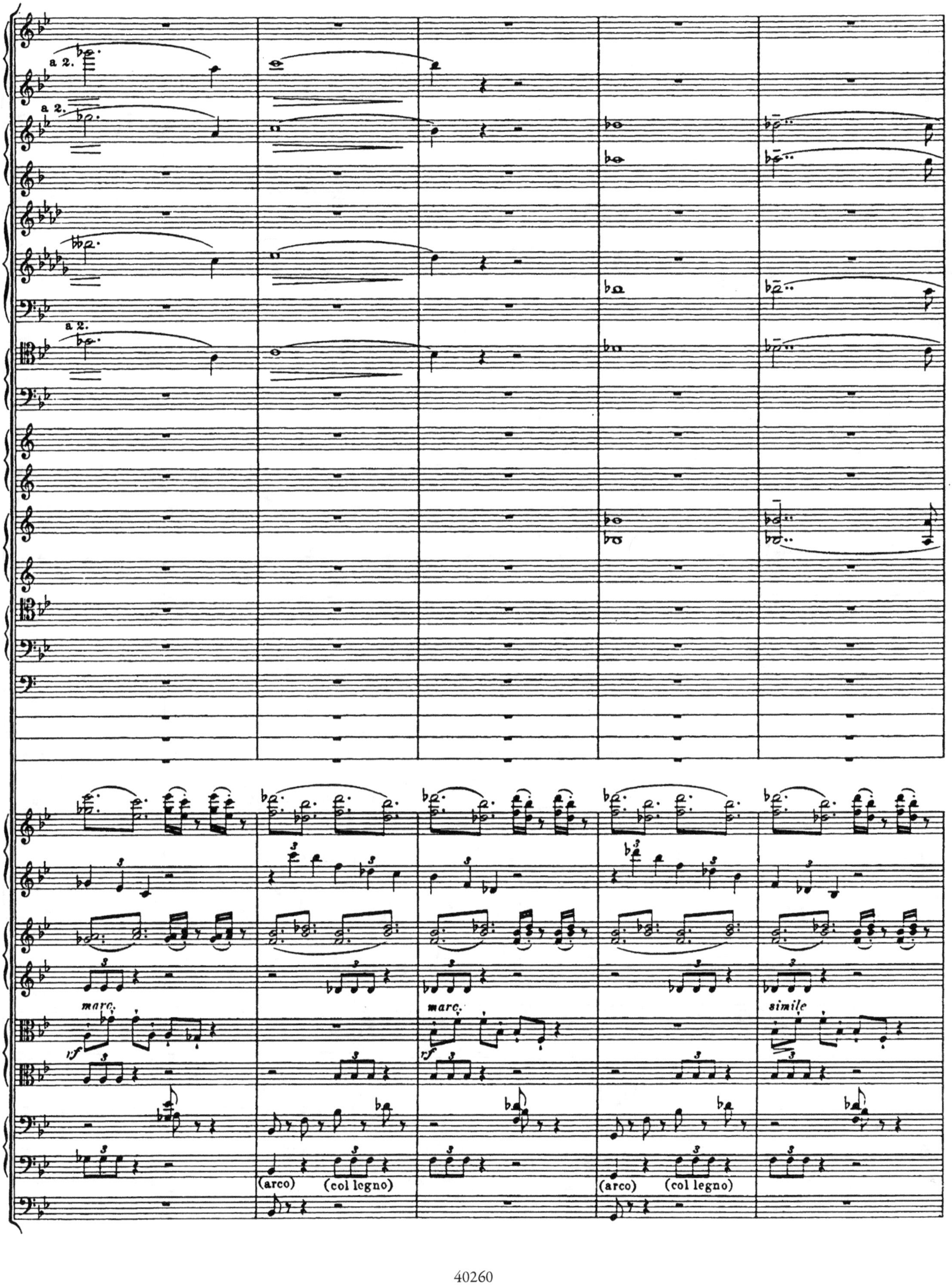
a 2.
a 2.
a 2.
marc.
rf
marc.
rf
simile
(arco)
(col legno)
(arco)
(col legno)

Muta in D.

(arco)   (col legno)

(arco)   (col legno)

(arco)   (col legno)

E
a 2.
a 2.
gemendo
gemendo
gemendo
gemendo
a 2.
(f)
(f)
a 2.
(f)
(arco)
(col legno)
(arco)
(col legno)
(arco)
(col legno)
E

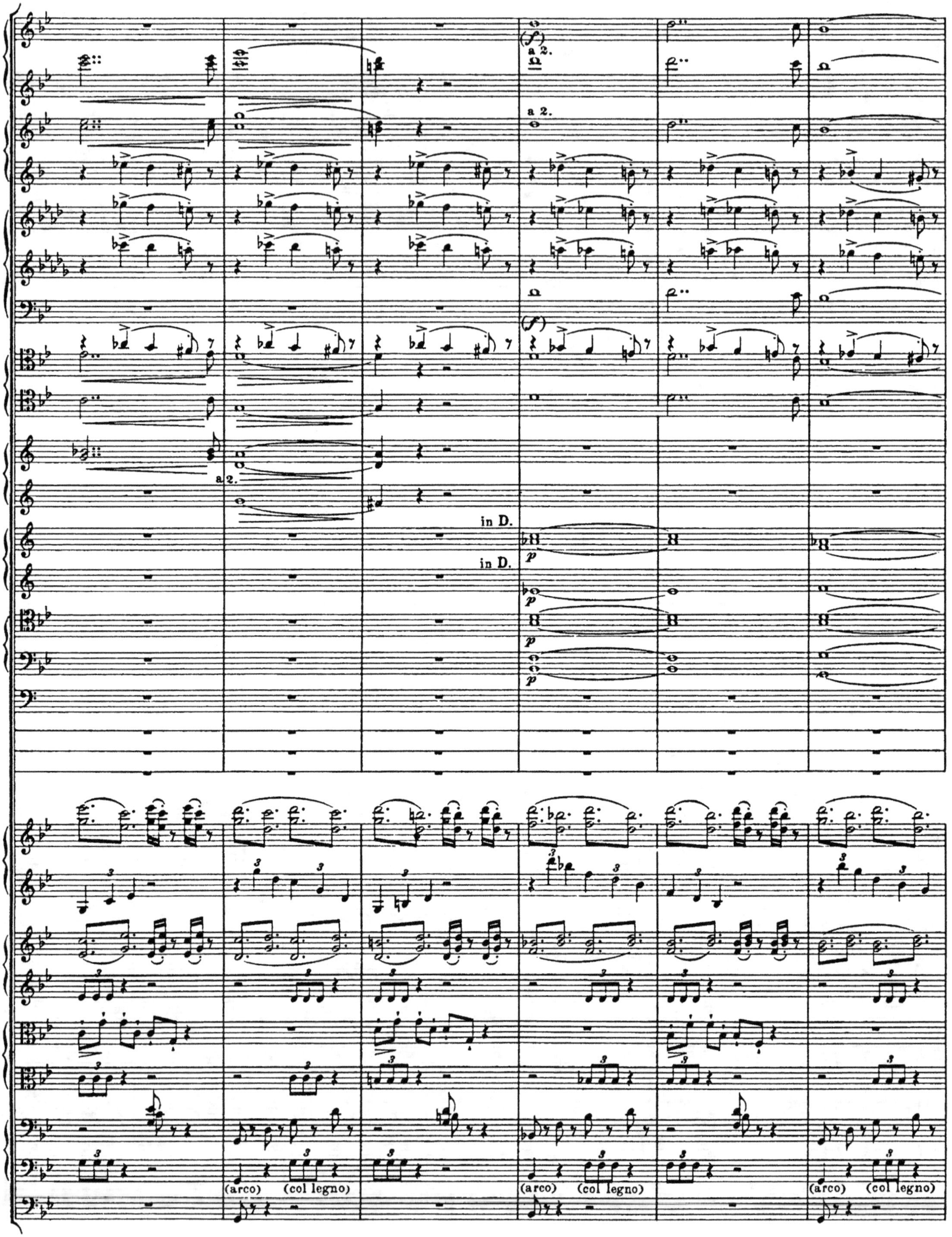
a 2.
a 2.
a 2.
in D.
in D.
(arco)
(col legno)
(arco)
(col legno)
(arco)
(col legno)

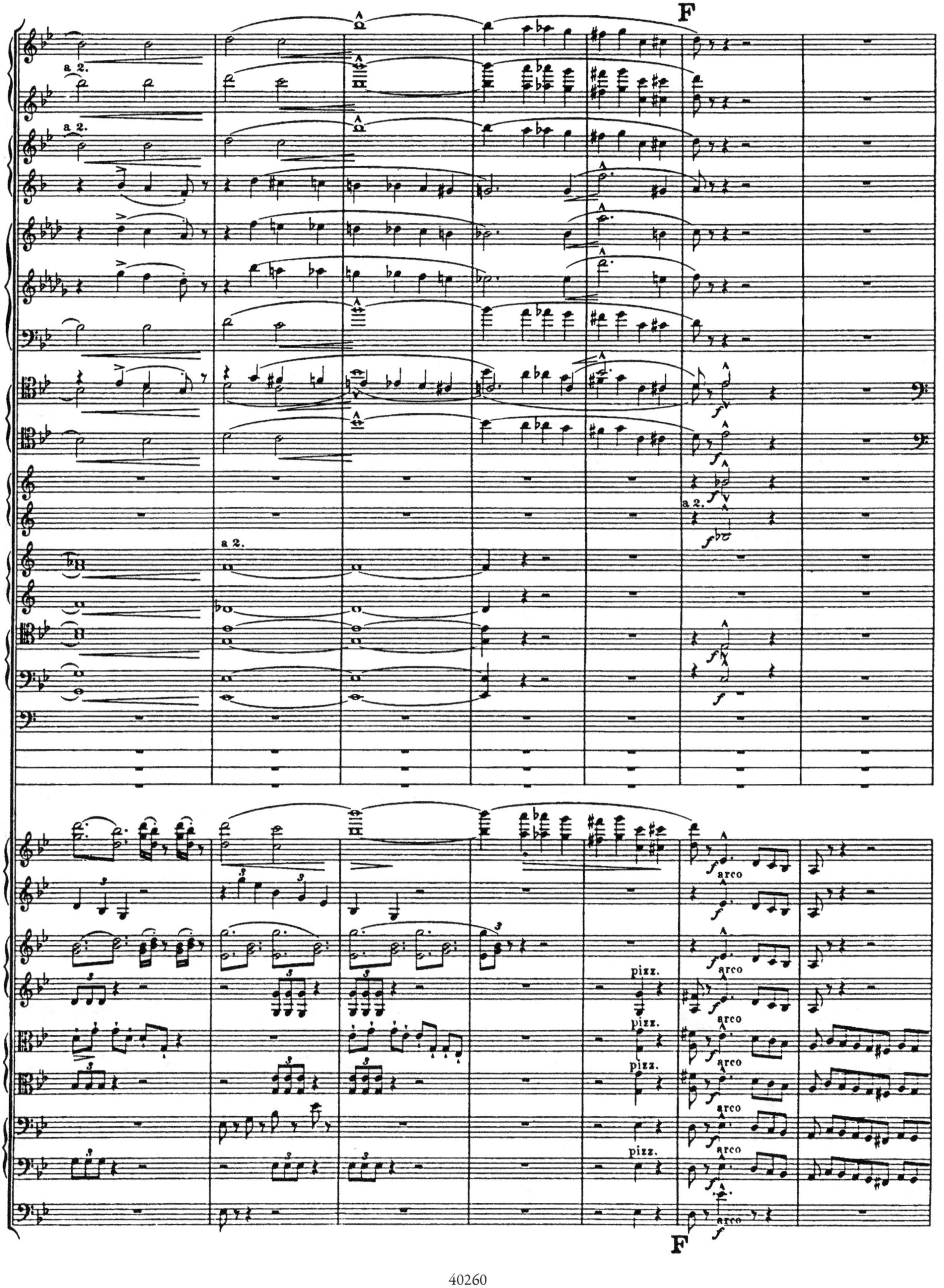
F
a 2.
a 2.
a 2.
a 2.
pizz.
arco
F

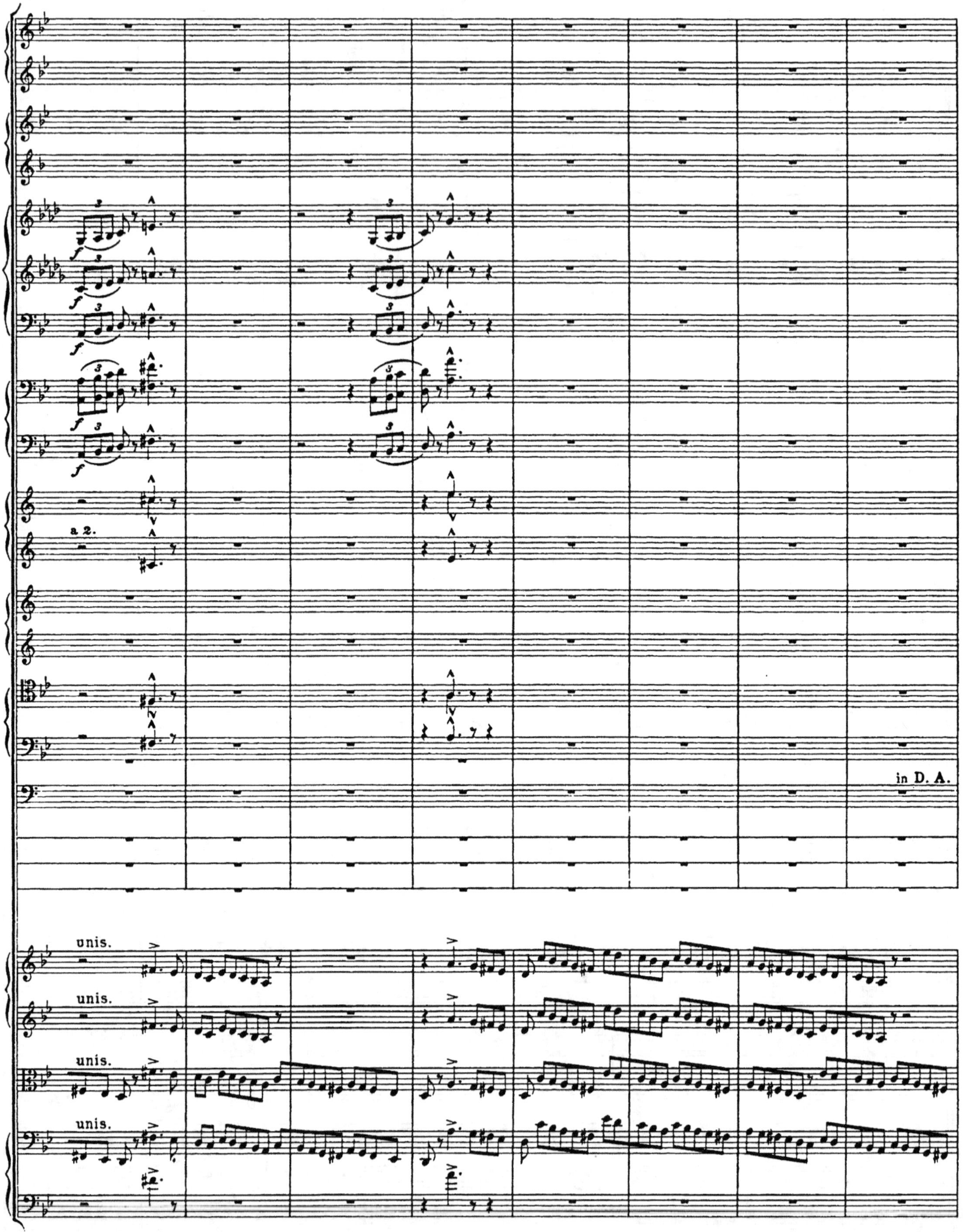
a 2.
in D. A.
unis.
unis.
unis.
unis.

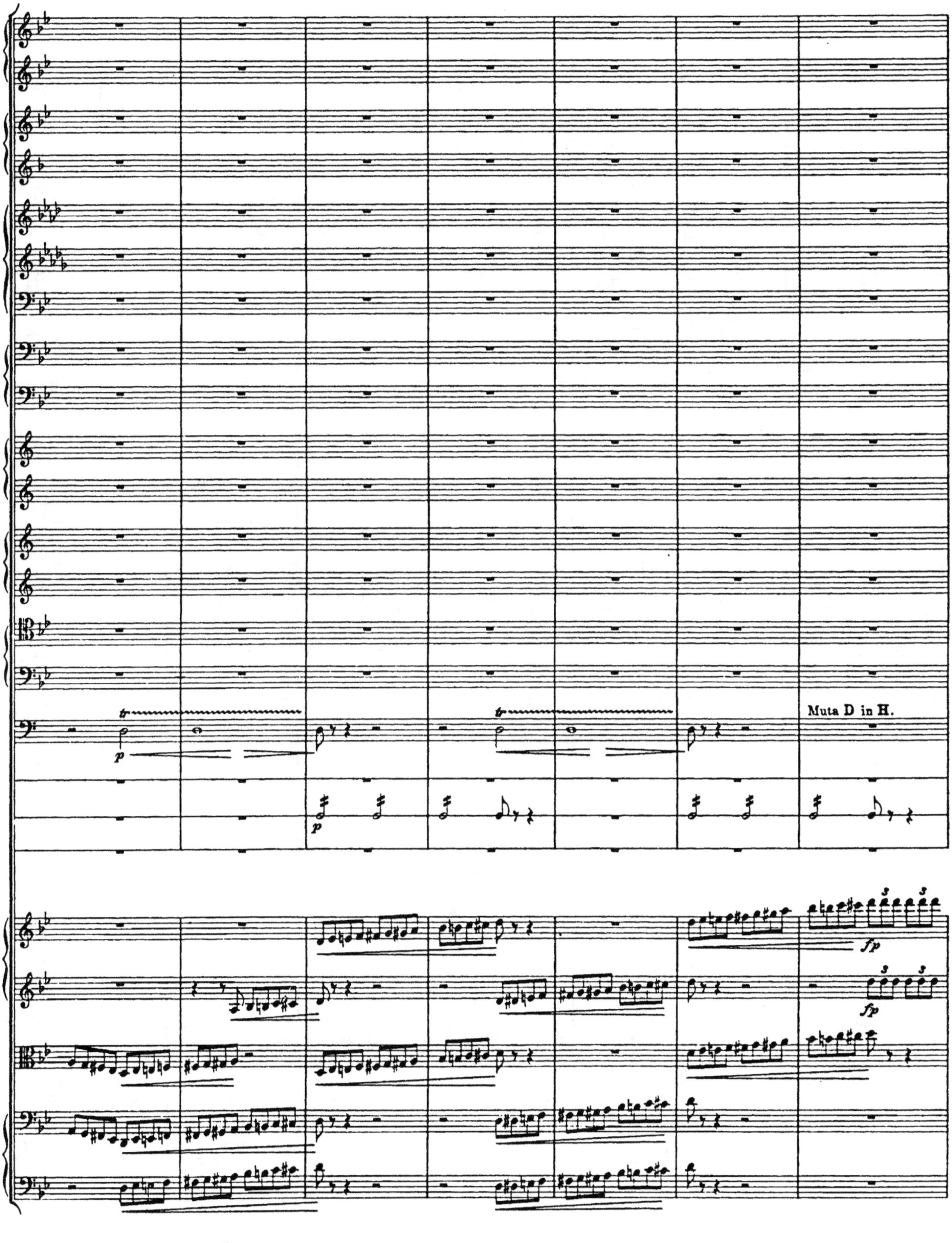
Muta D in H.

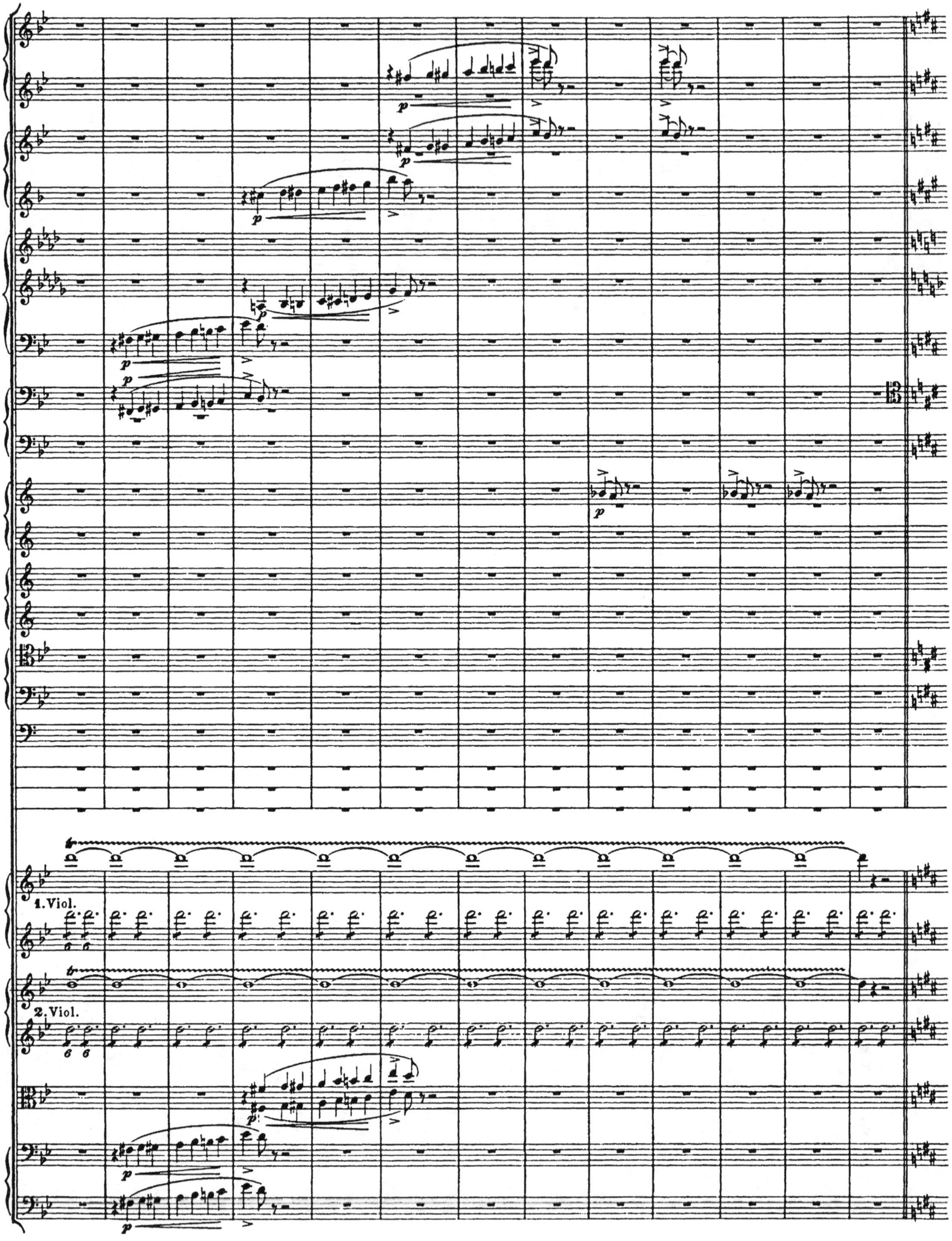
1. Viol.
2. Viol.

*) Zwei einzelne Violinen.
Two violins soli.
Deux violons seuls.

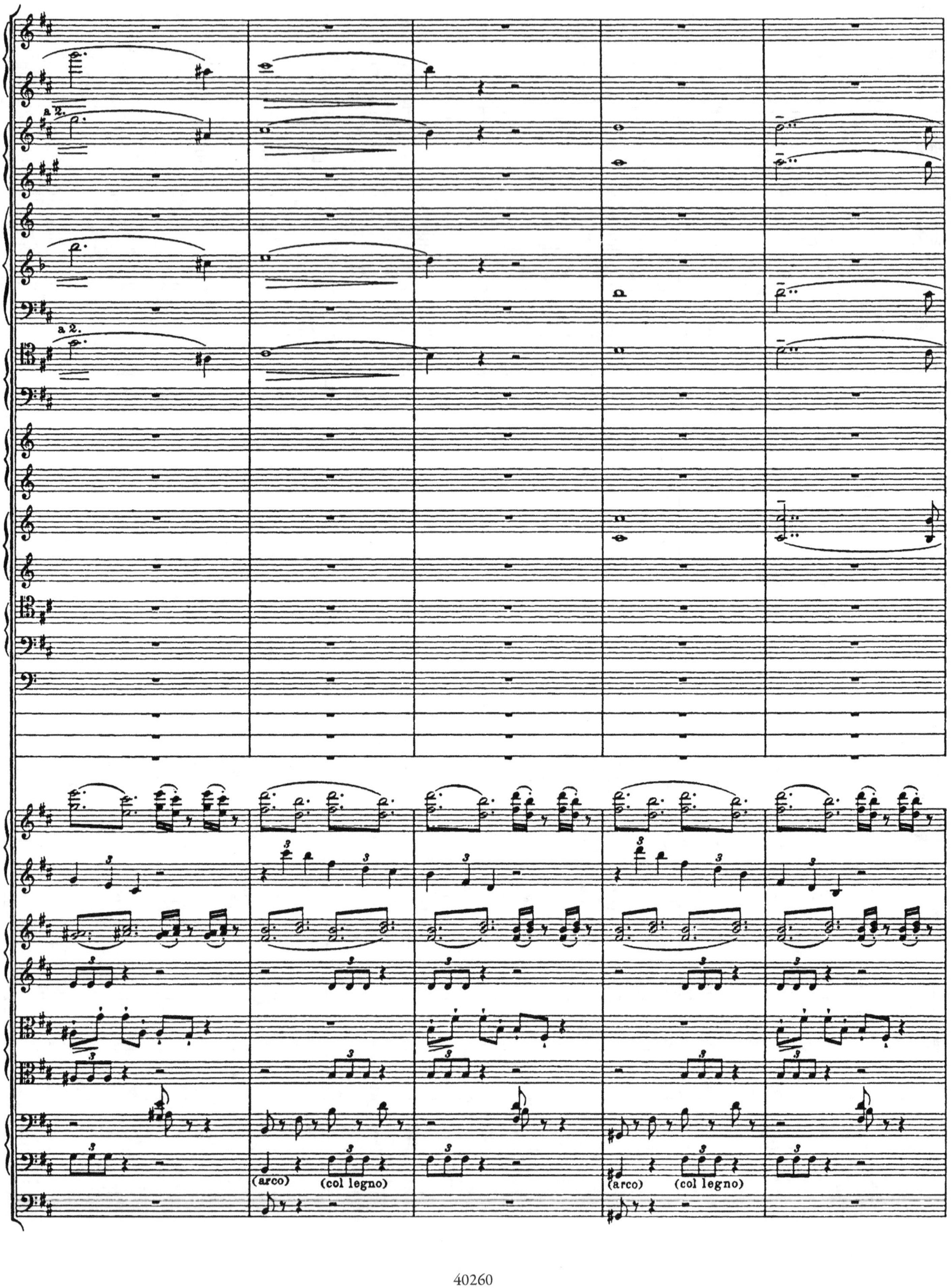
a 2.
a 2.
(arco)
(col legno)
(arco)
(col legno)

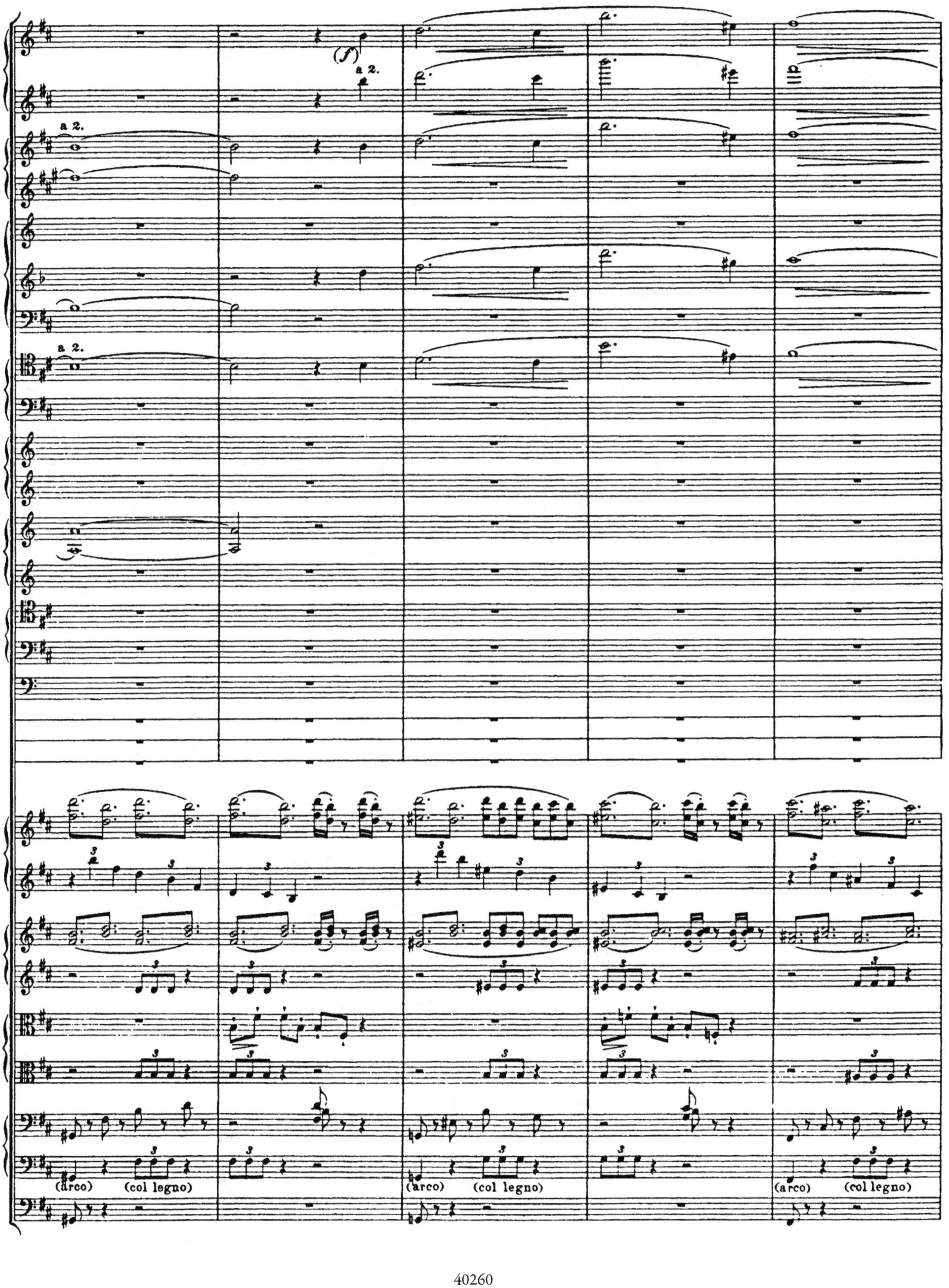
(f)
a 2.
a 2.
a 2.
(arco)
(col legno)
(arco)
(col legno)
(arco)
(col legno)

G
a 2.
a 2.
(gemendo)
(gemendo)
(gemendo)
(gemendo)
a 2.
(f)
(f)
a 2.
(f)
arco
(arco)
(col legno)
(arco)
(col legno)
G

a 2.
pizz.
arco
pizz.
(arco)
(col legno)
(arco)
(col legno)
(arco)
(col legno)

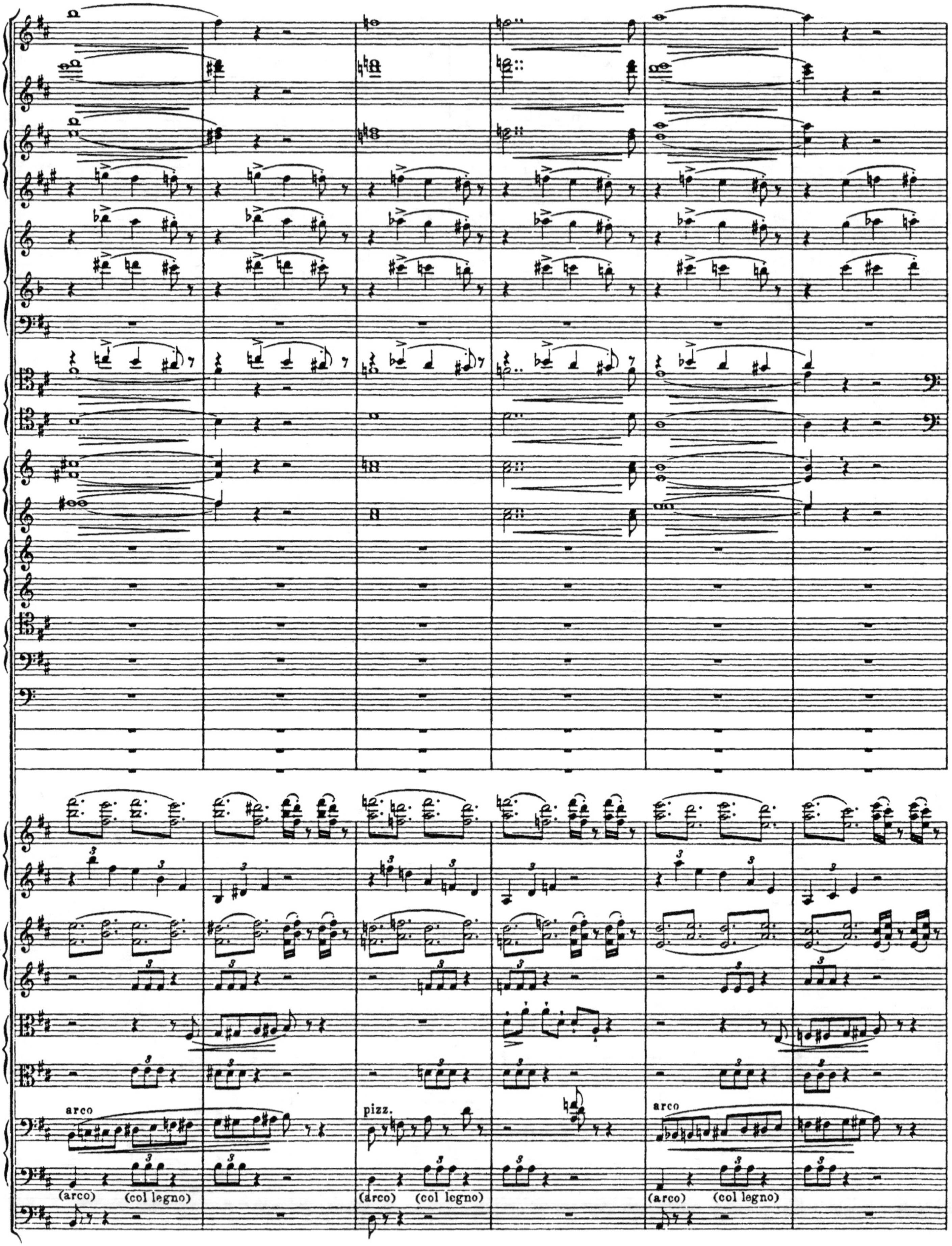
arco
pizz.
arco
(arco)
(col legno)
(arco)
(col legno)
(arco)
(col legno)

H

*) Erste Viol. a 2 Parti.
First Vln. in 2 Parts.
Premiers Viol. en 2 parties.

Zweite Viol. a 3 Parti.
Second Vln. in 3 Parts.
Seconds Viol. en 3 parties.

H

tr
a 2.
f marc.
a 2. f marc.
a 2. f marc.
a 2.
a 2.
(f) marc.
(f) marc.
poco cresc.
p
(f) marc.
(f) marc.

tr
a 2.
a 2.
f marc.
f marc.
a 2.
f marc.
a 2.
f marc.
a 2.
f marc.
(p)
(p)
tr
pp
poco cresc.

a 2.
a 2.
a 2.
a 2.
Muta H in D.
1. Viol.
arco
2. Viol.
arco
Bratsch.
div.
non div.
div.

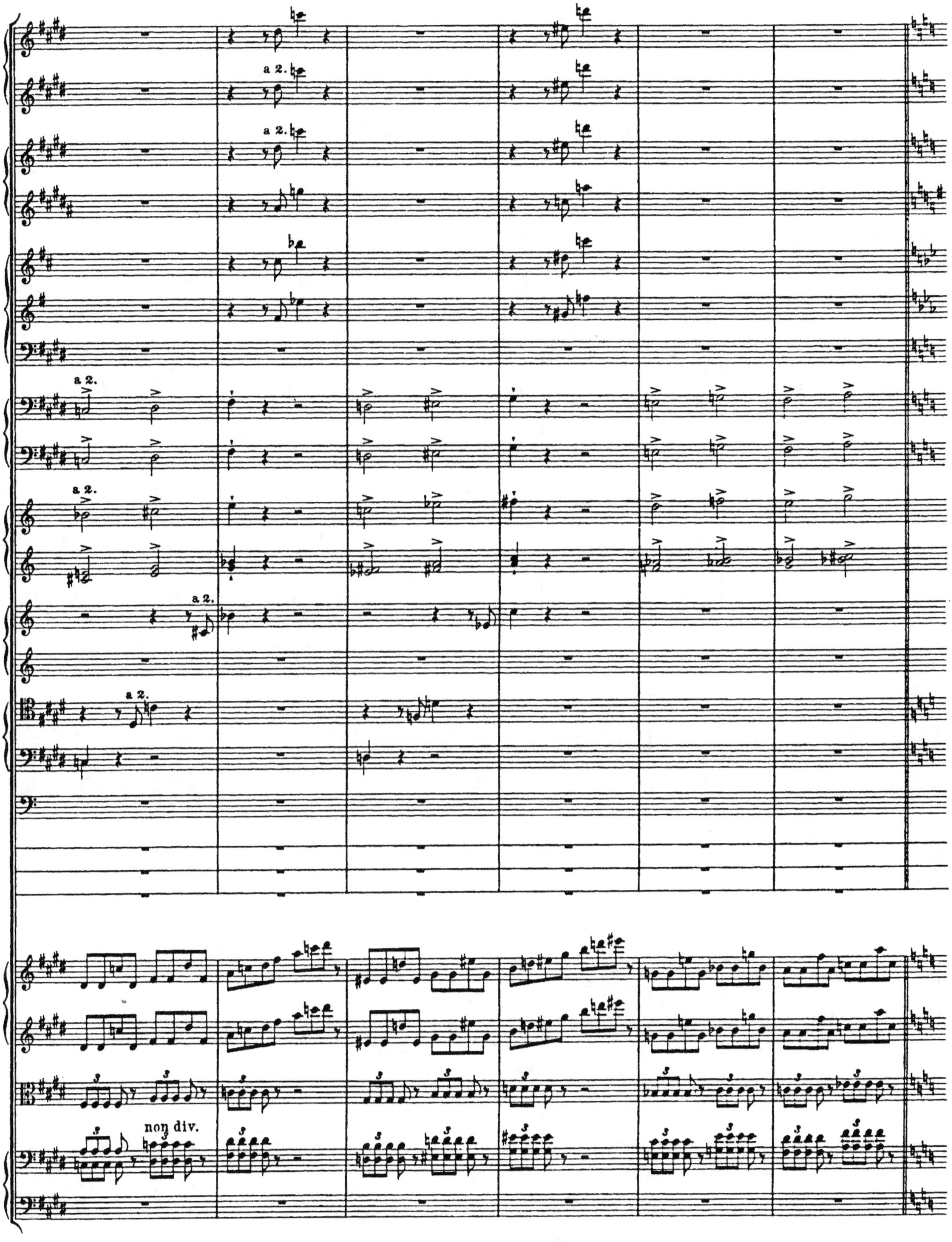
a 2.
a 2.
a 2.
a 2.
a 2.
a 2.
non div.

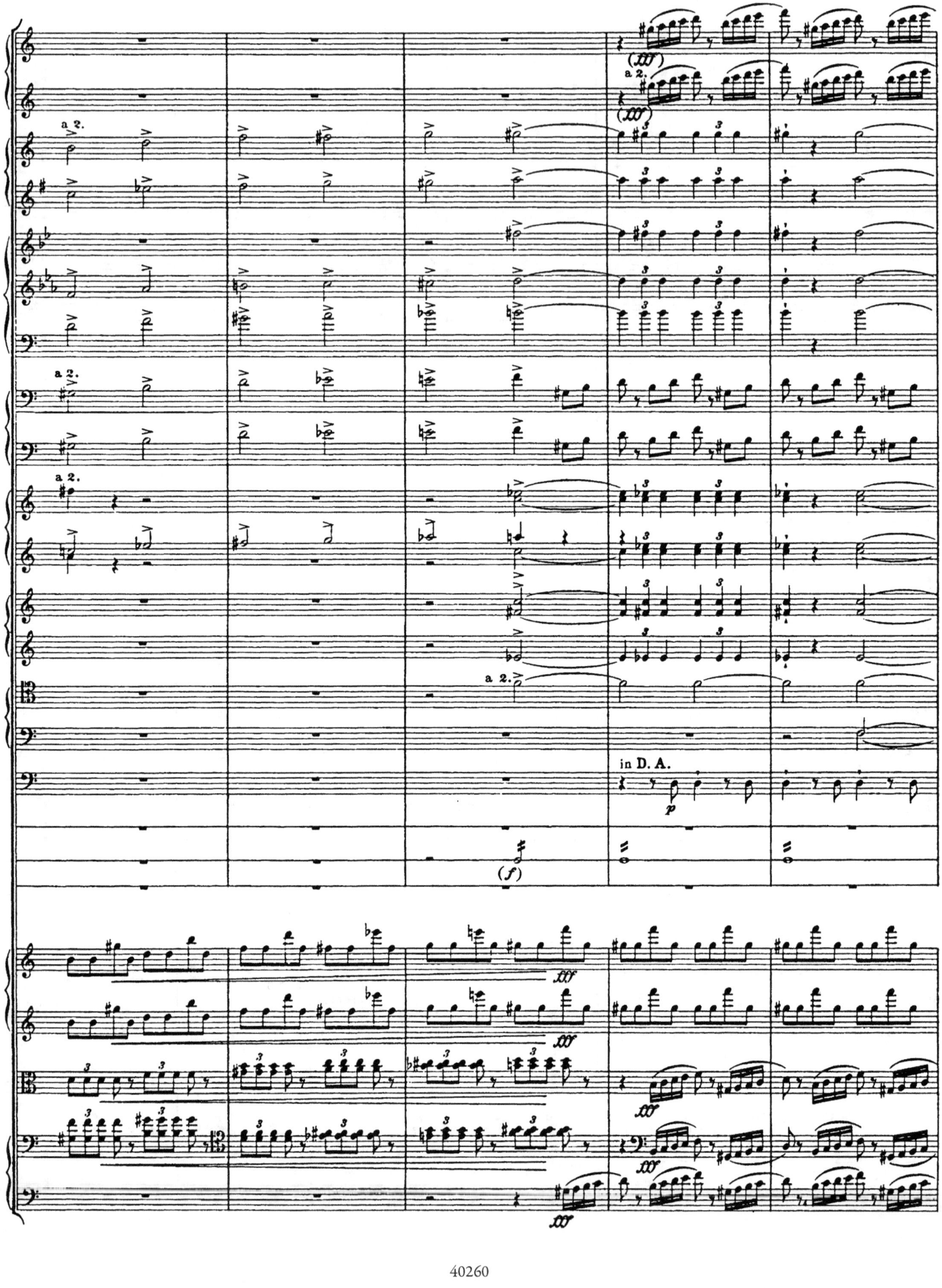
(fff)
a 2.
(fff)
a 2.
a 2.
a 2.
a 2.
in D. A.
p
(f)
fff
fff
fff
fff
fff

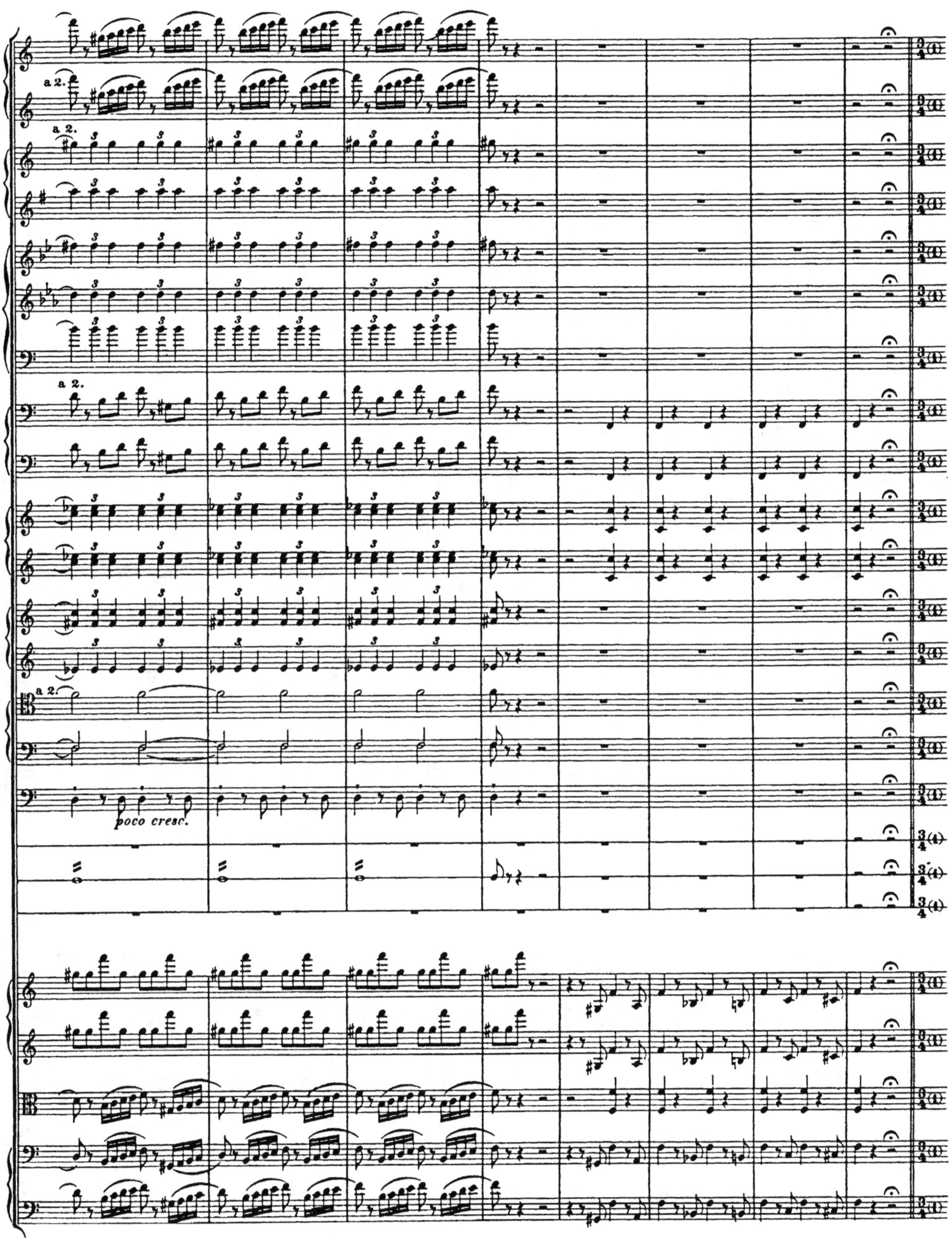
a 2.
a 2.
a 2.
a 2.
poco cresc.

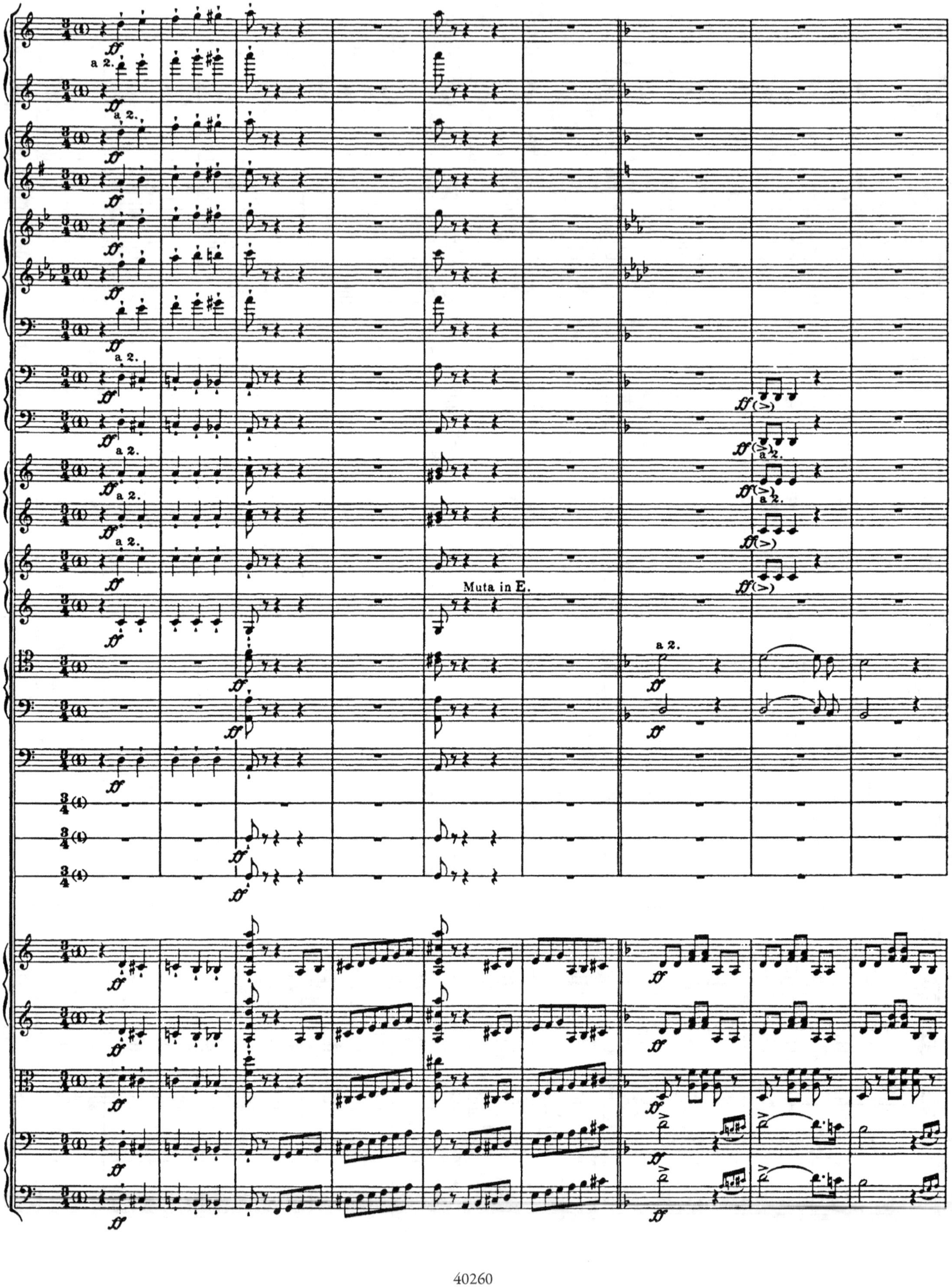
a 2.
Muta in E.

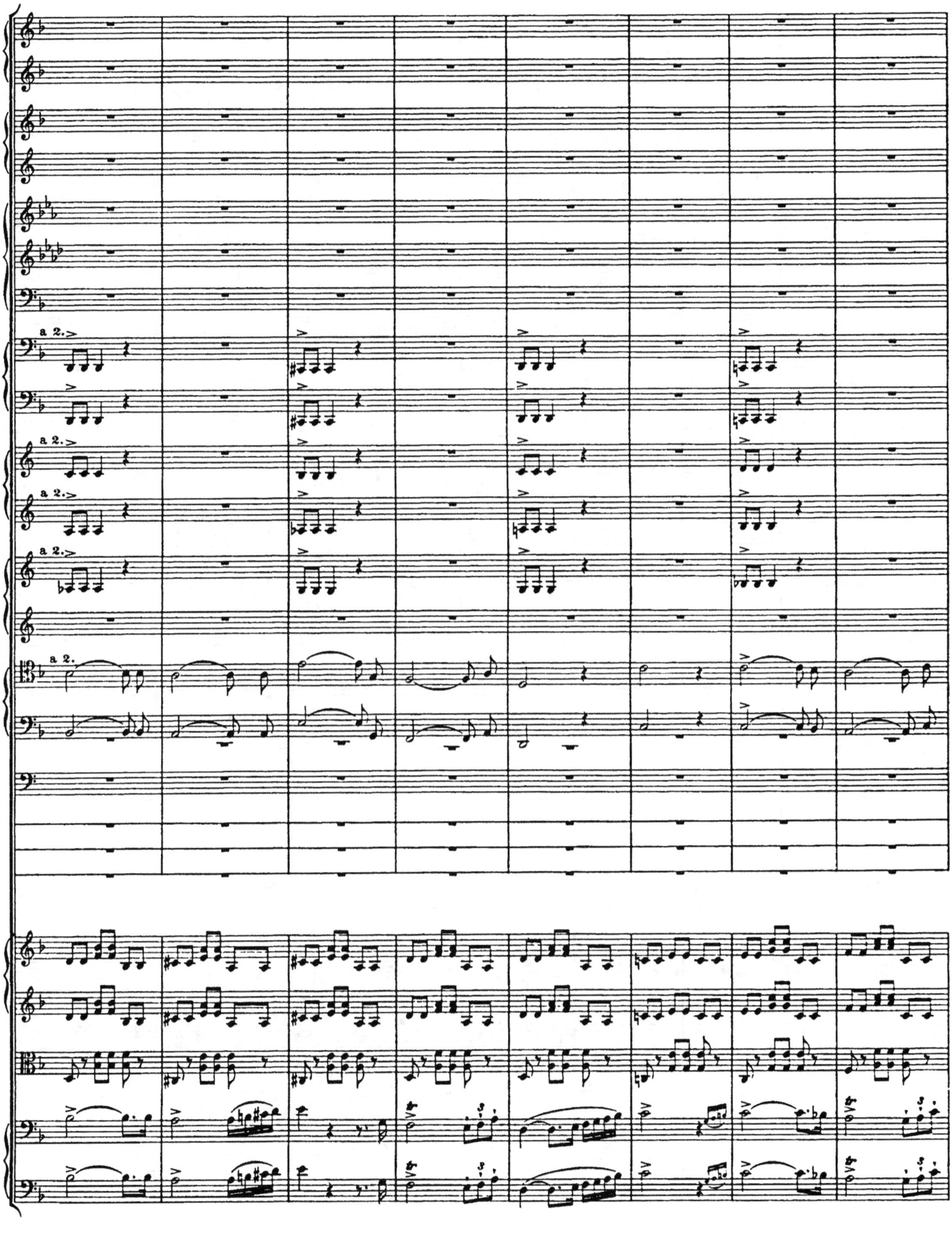
a 2.
a 2.
a 2.
a 2.
a 2.

*) Die Zeichen ×× bedeuten pizzicato.
×× *signify pizzicato.*
×× *signifient pizzicato.*

40260

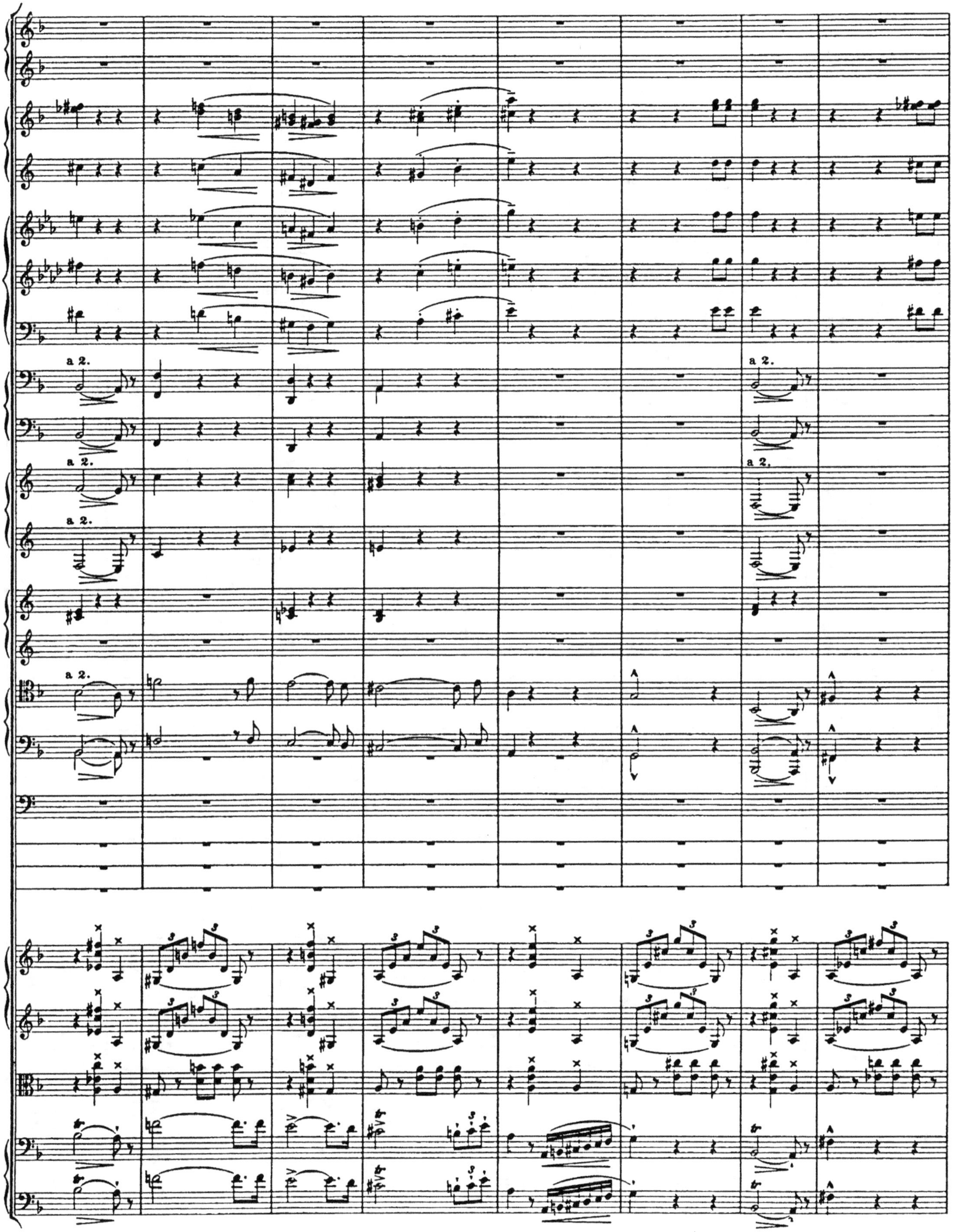
a 2.
a 2.
a 2.
a 2.
a 2.
a 2.
a 2.
tr
tr
tr
tr

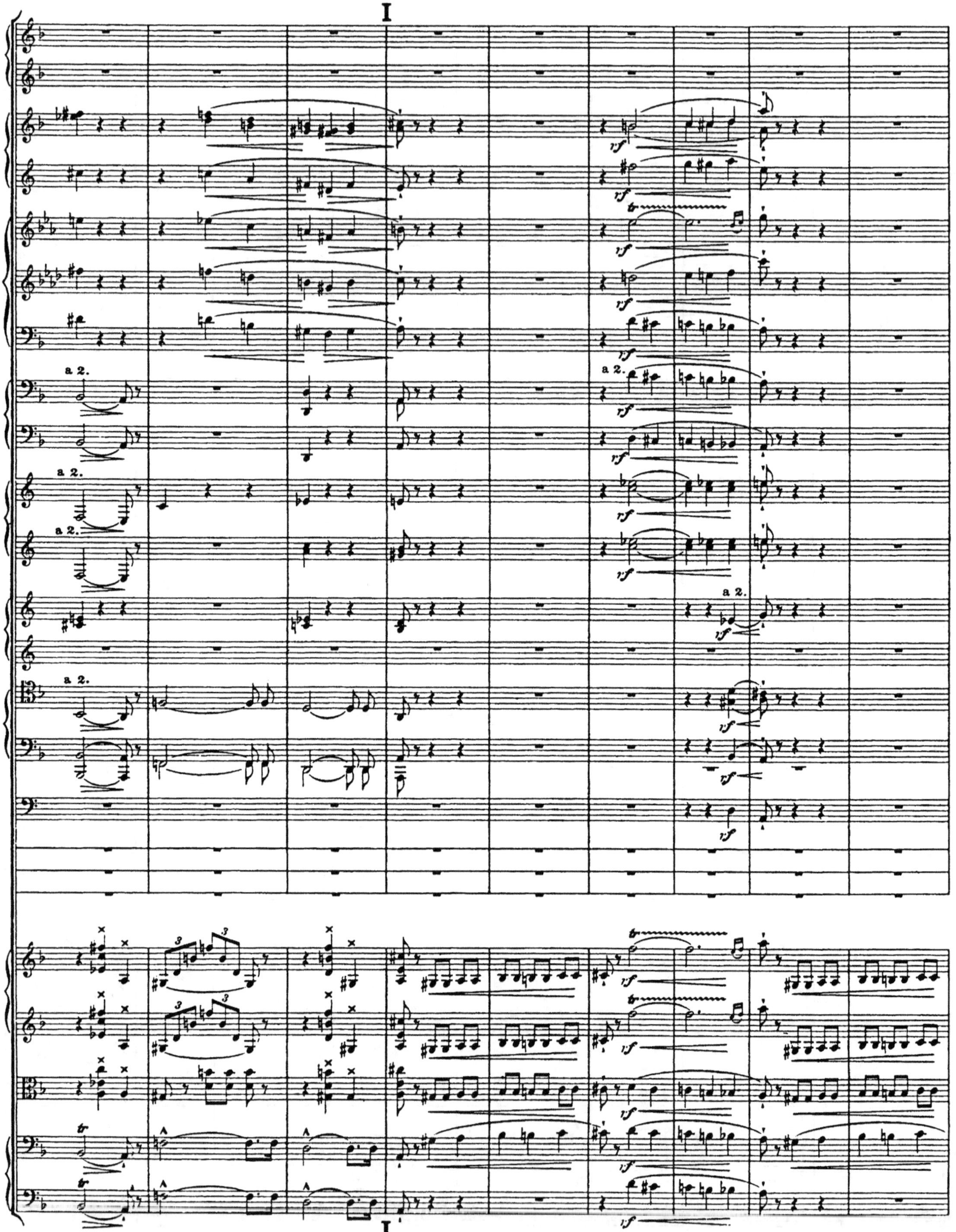
I
a 2.
a 2.
a 2.
a 2.
a 2.
a 2.
rf
tr
I

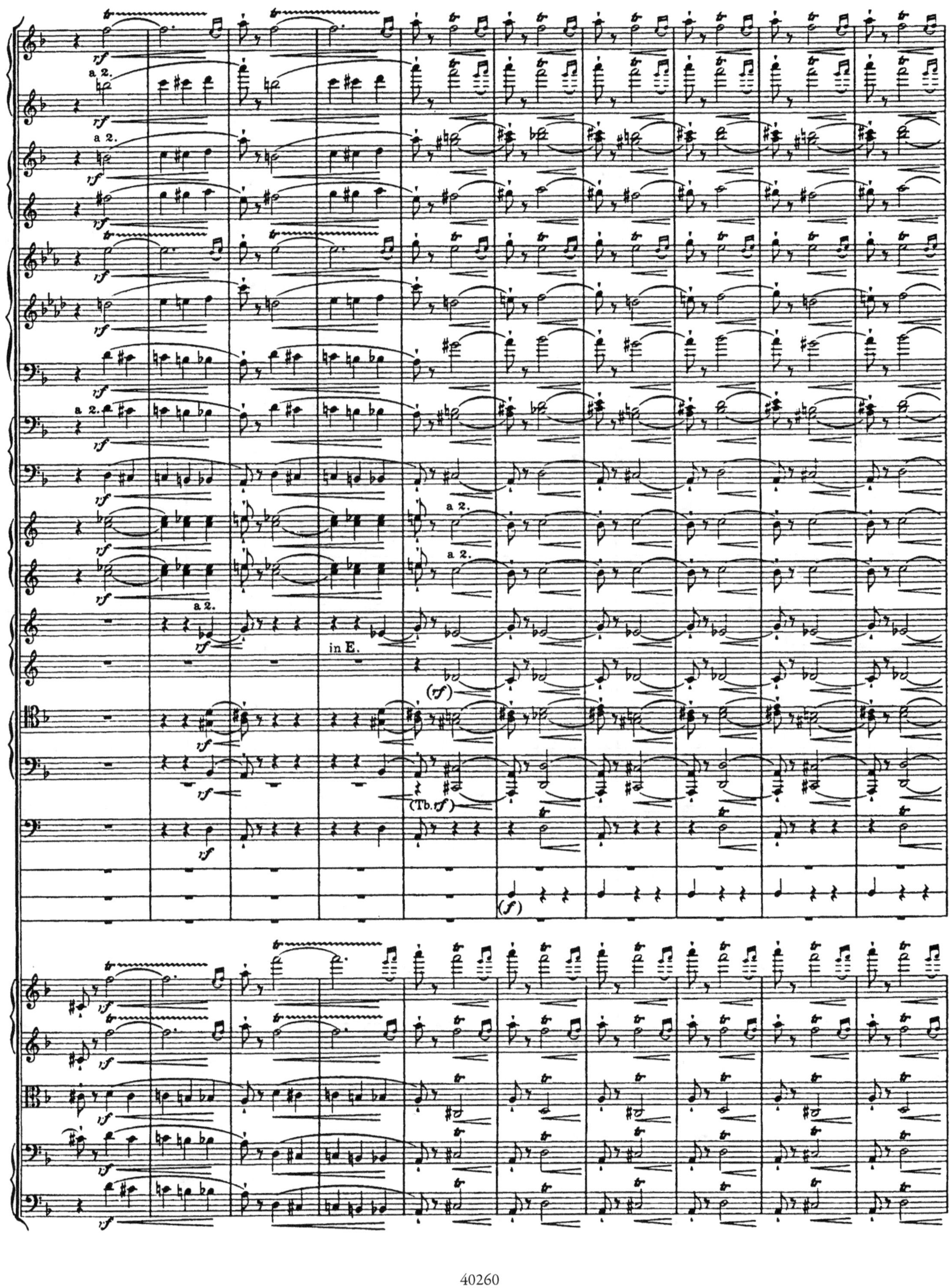
a 2.
in E.
(rf)
(Tb. rf)
(f)

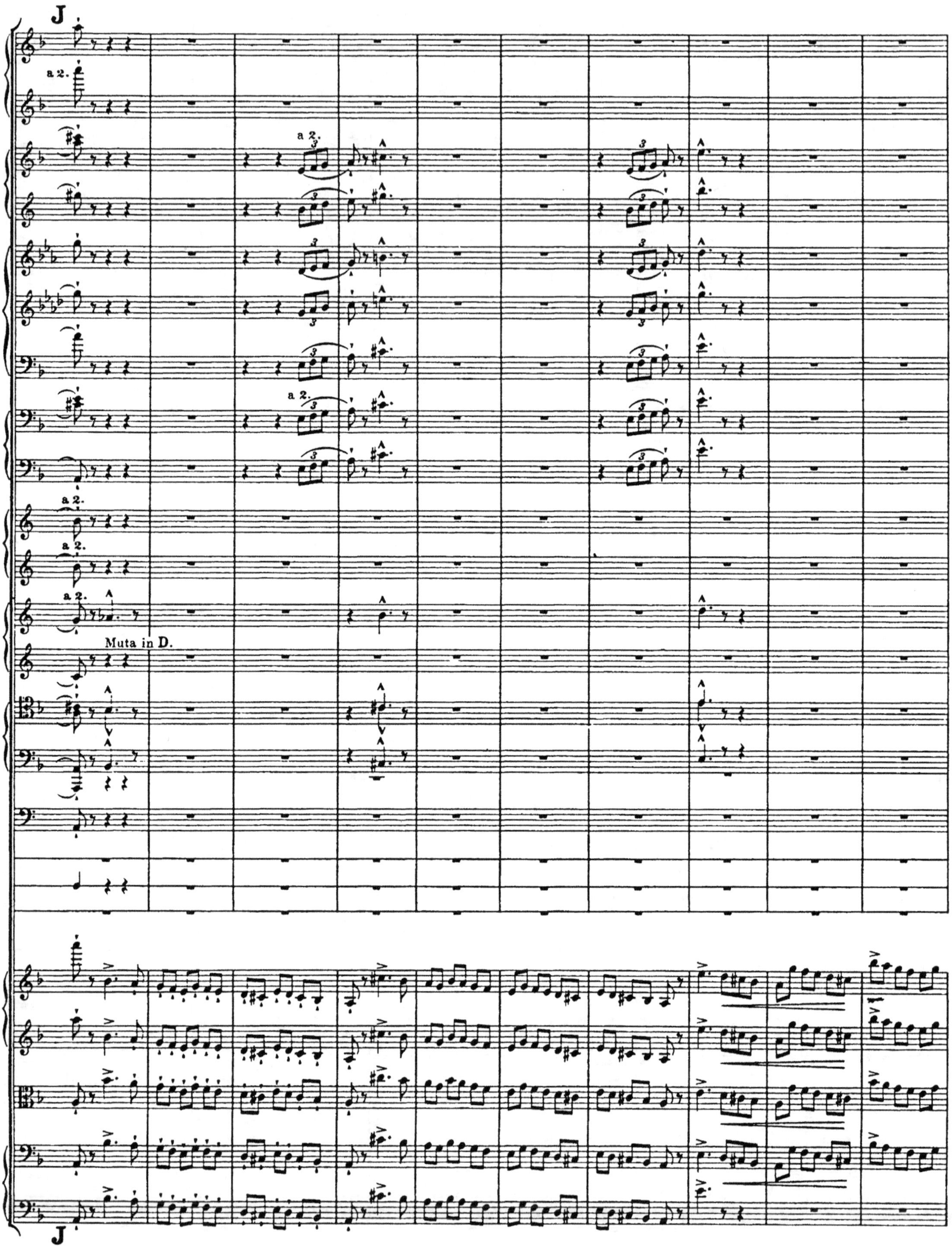
J
a 2.
a 2.
a 2.
a 2.
a 2.
a 2.
Muta in D.
J

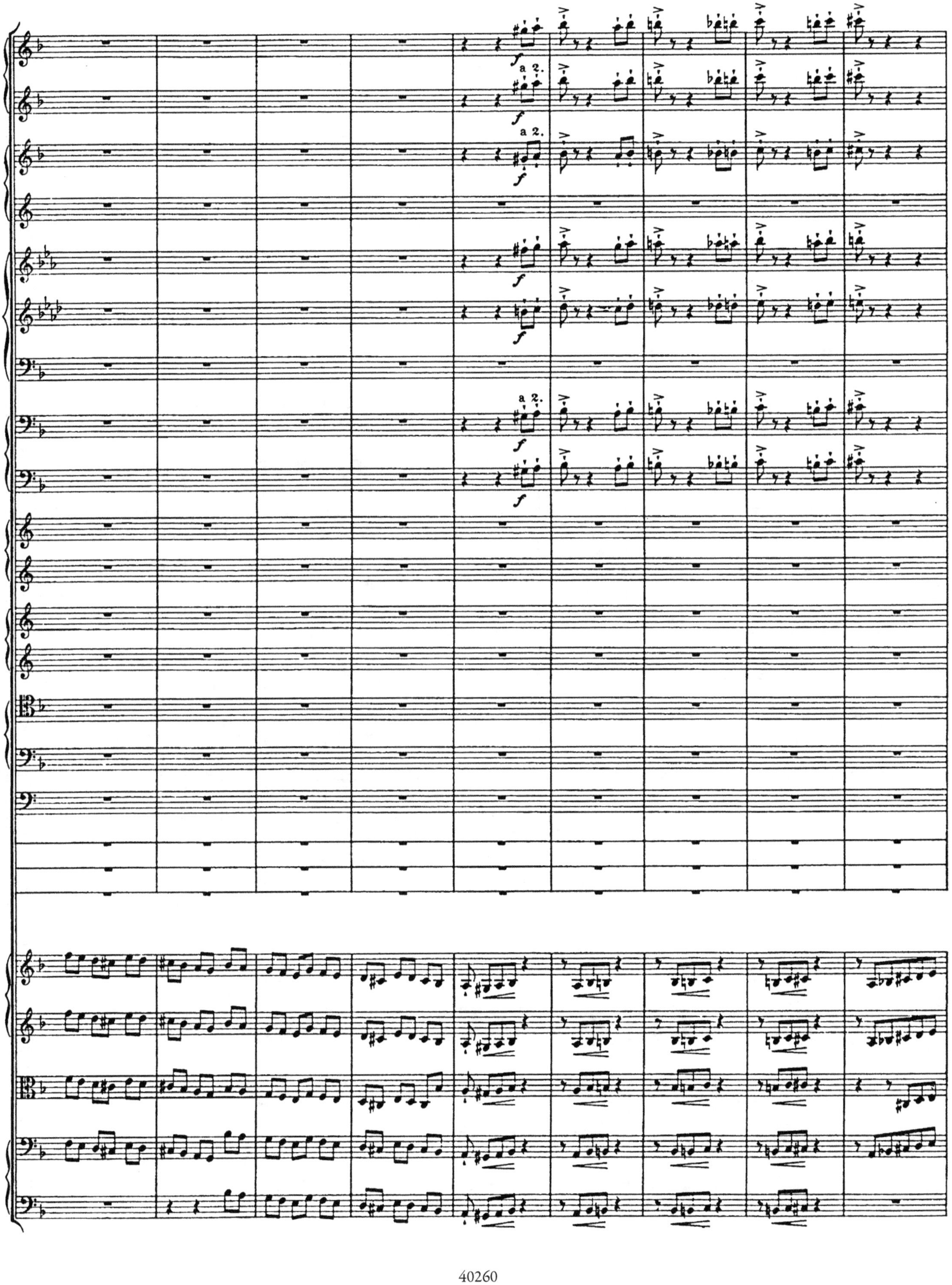
a 2.
a 2.
a 2.
f
f
f
f
f
f
f
f

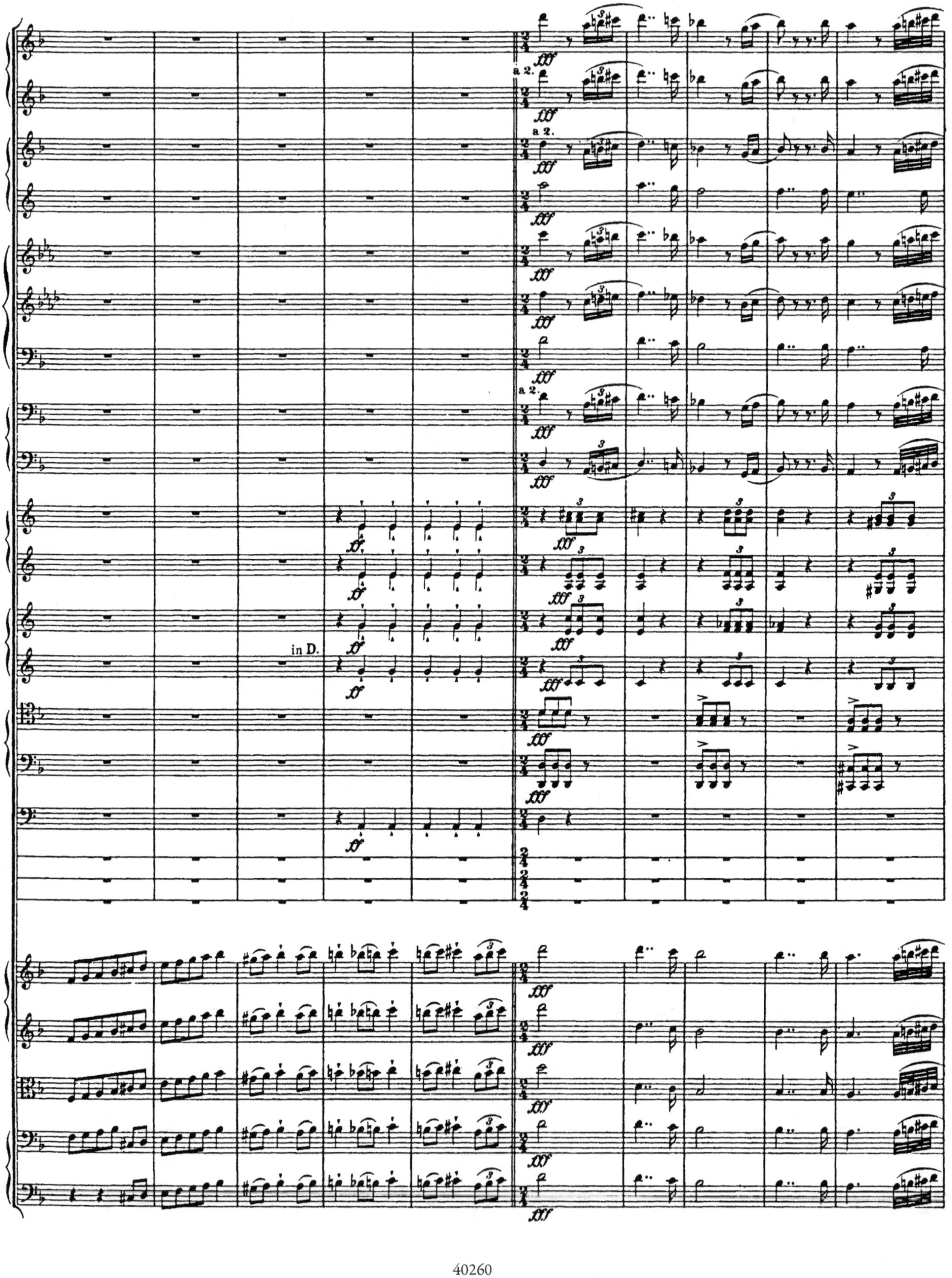
a 2.
a 2.
a 2.
in D.

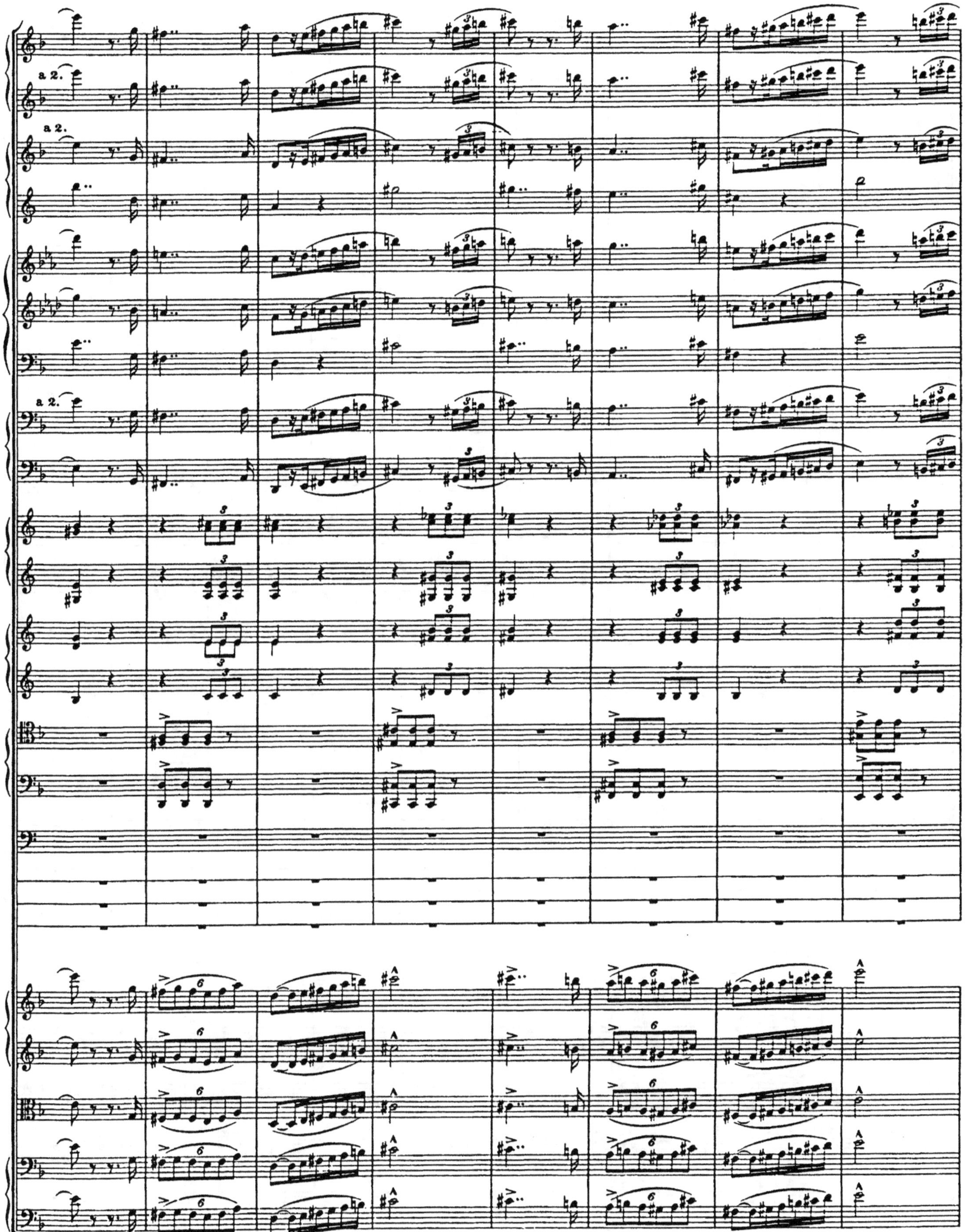
a 2.
a 2.
a 2.

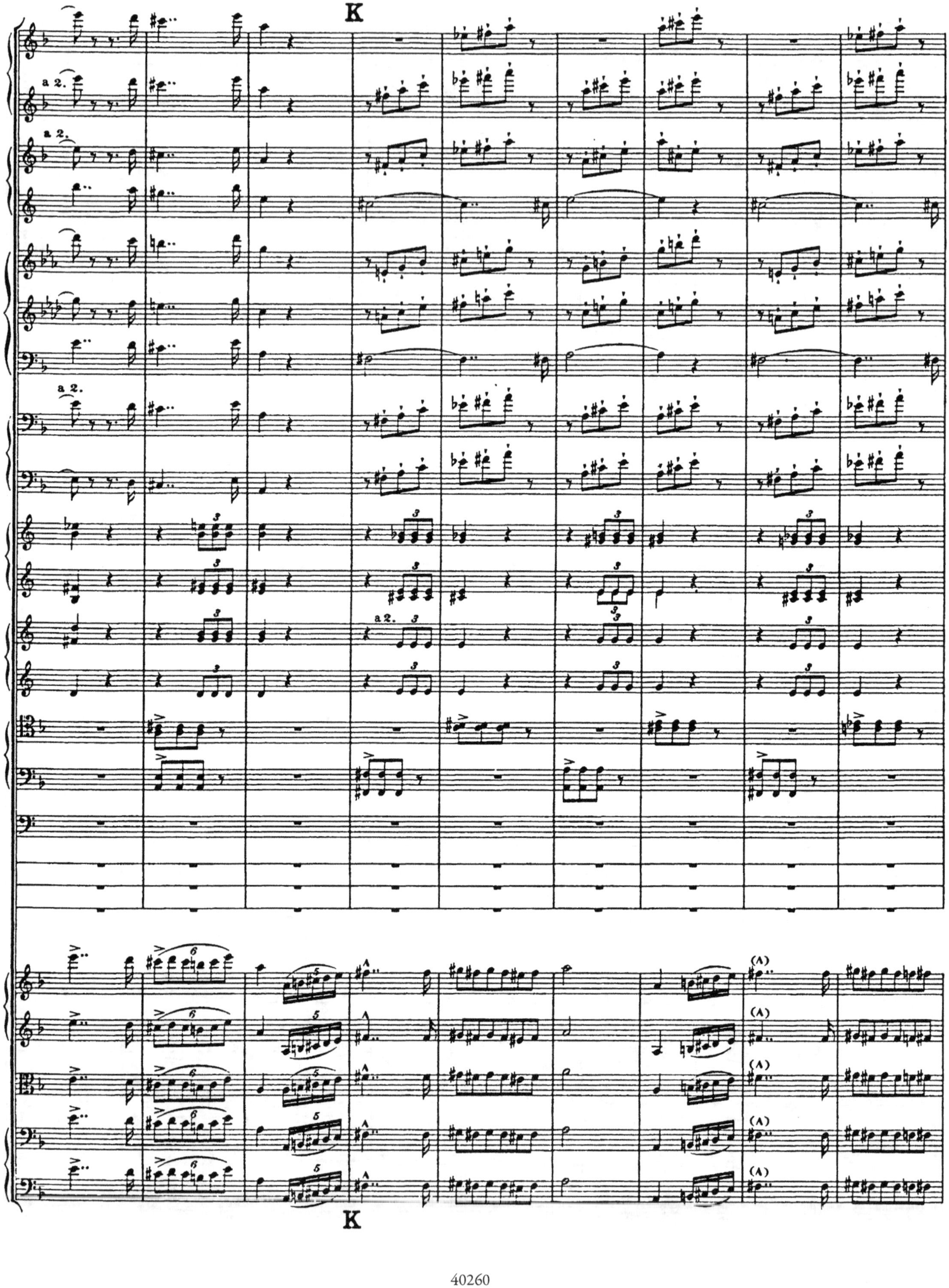
K
a 2.
a 2.
a 2.
a 2.
(A)
K

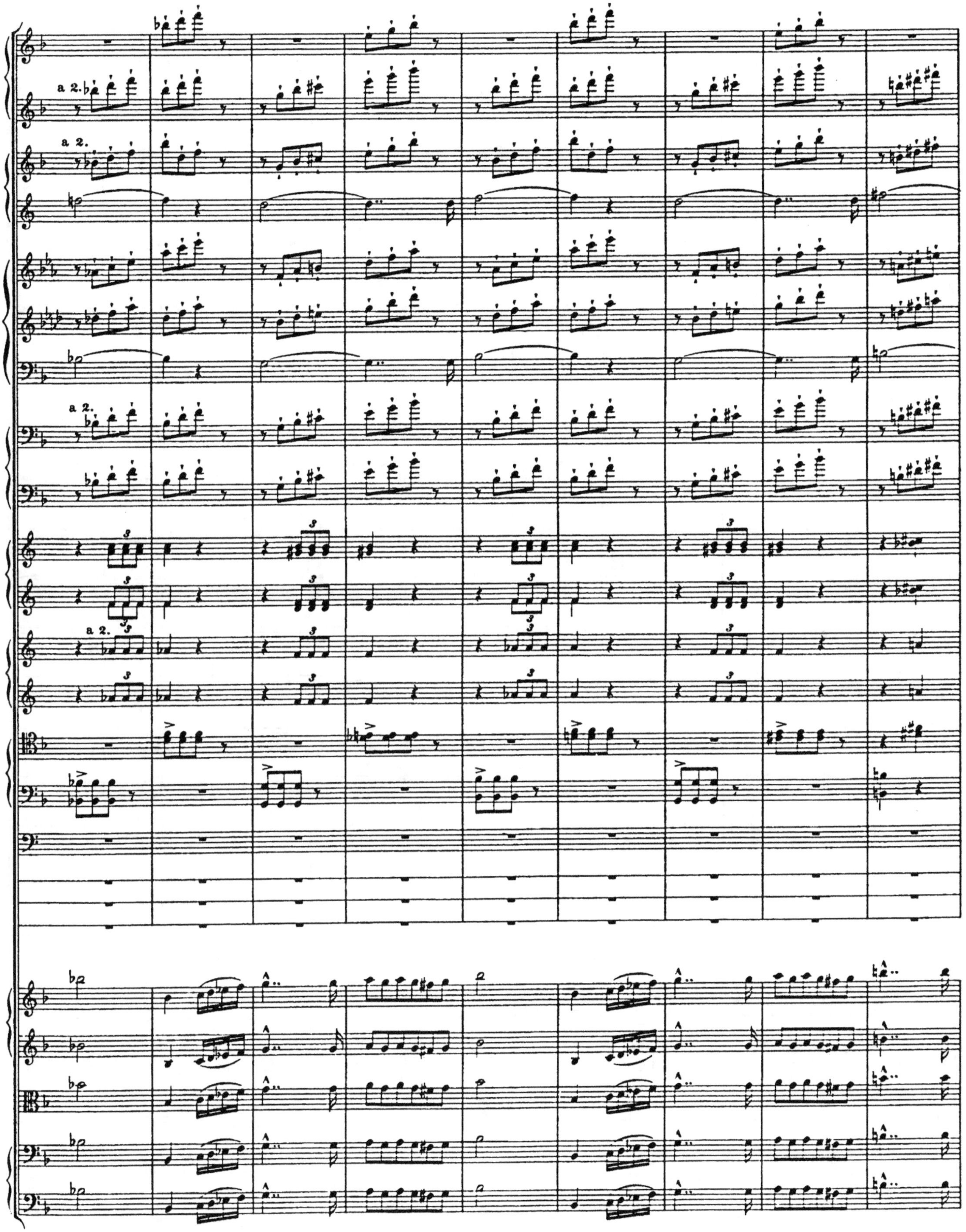
a 2.
a 2.
a 2.
a 2.

68

40260

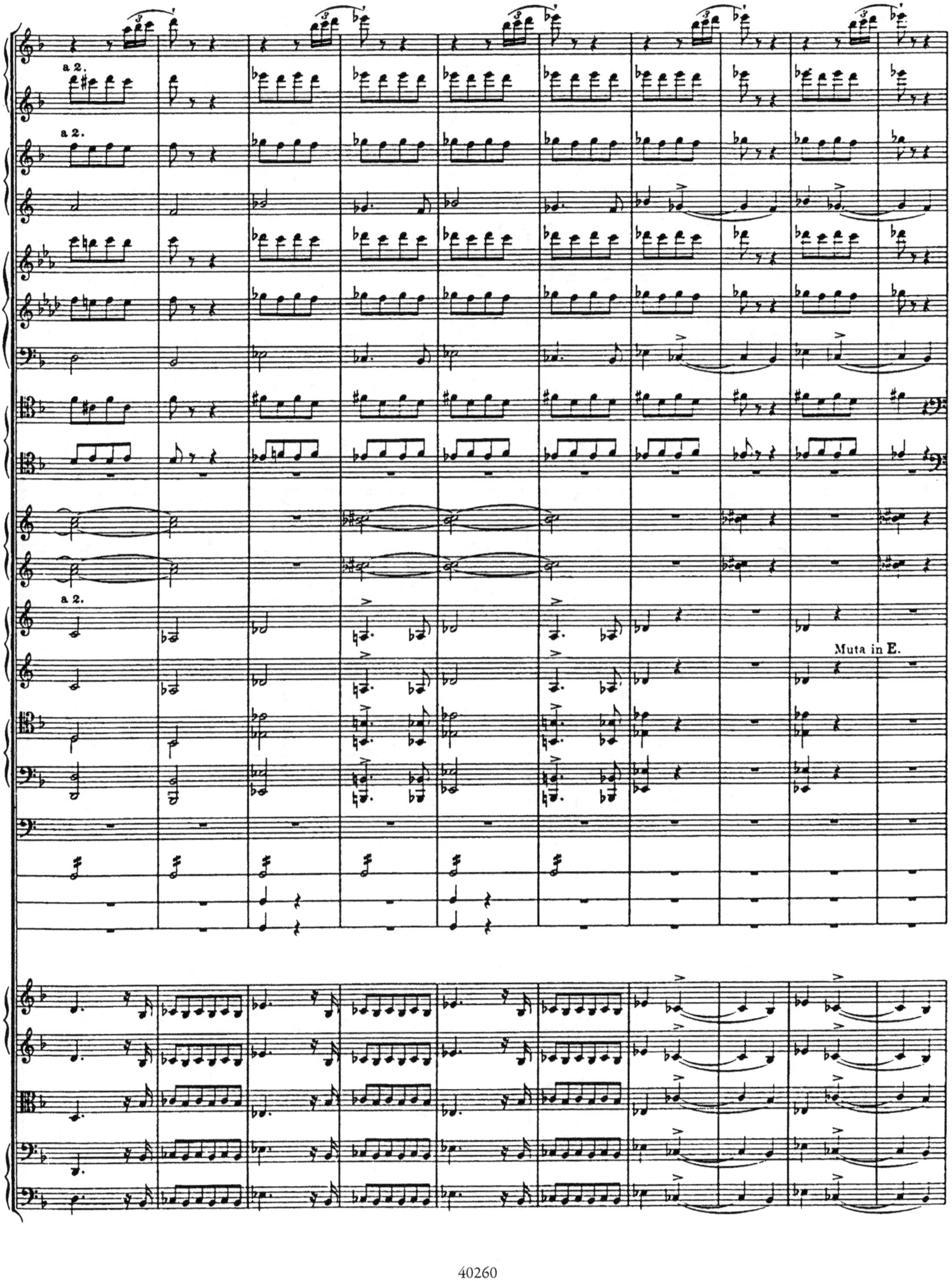
a 2.
a 2.
a 2.
Muta in E.

a 2.
poco ritenuto
(ff)
poco a poco rallentando
1. 2. Fag.
a 2.
3. Fag.
f
p
ff

Andante.

Andante.

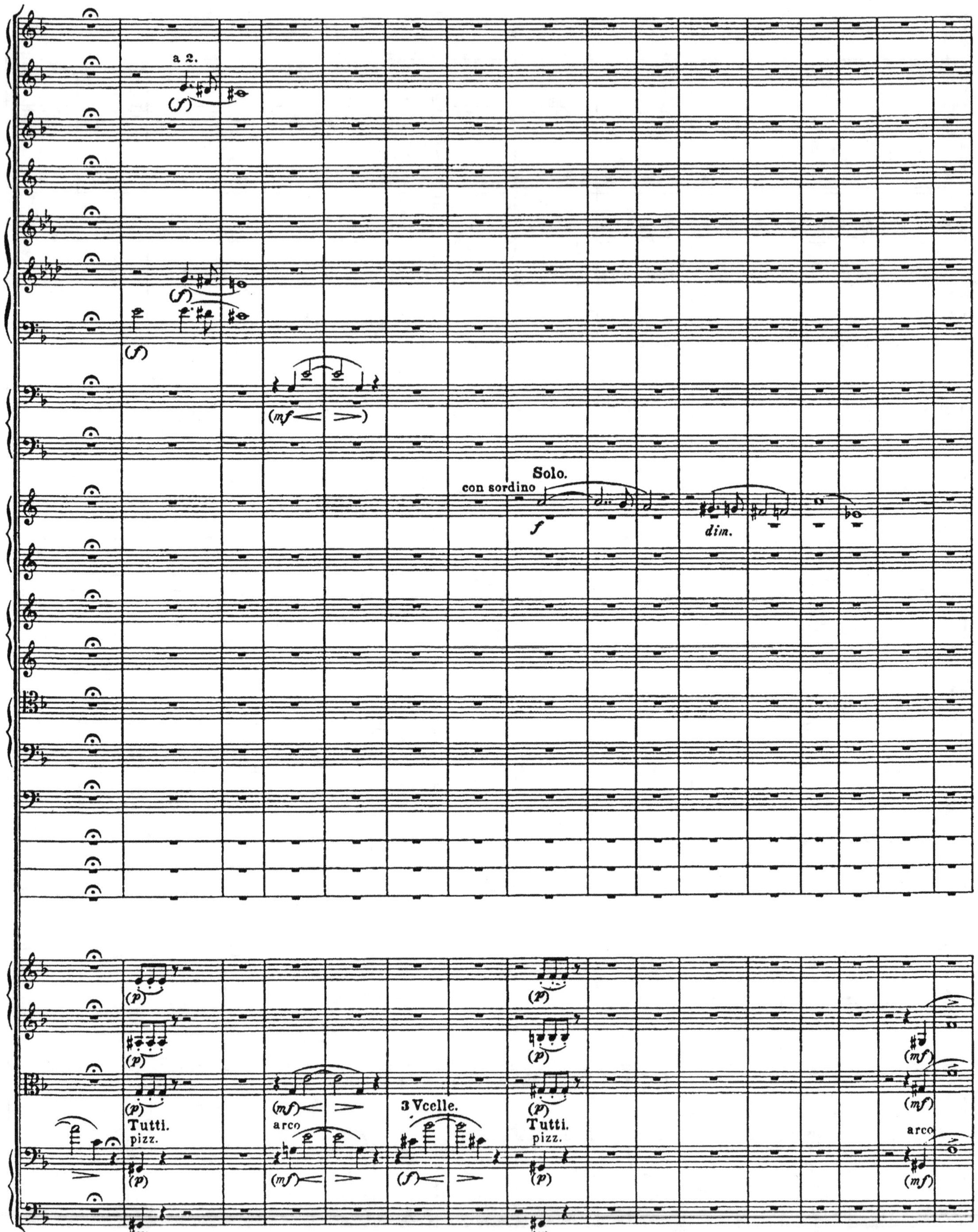
a 2.
Solo.
con sordino
dim.
3 Vcelle.
Tutti.
pizz.
arco

Allegro.
in E.
(f) marziale, nobile
tremolo
poco ritenuto
tremolo
poco ritenuto
arco
(dim.)
poco ritenuto
(mf)
(dim.)
(p)
Allegro.

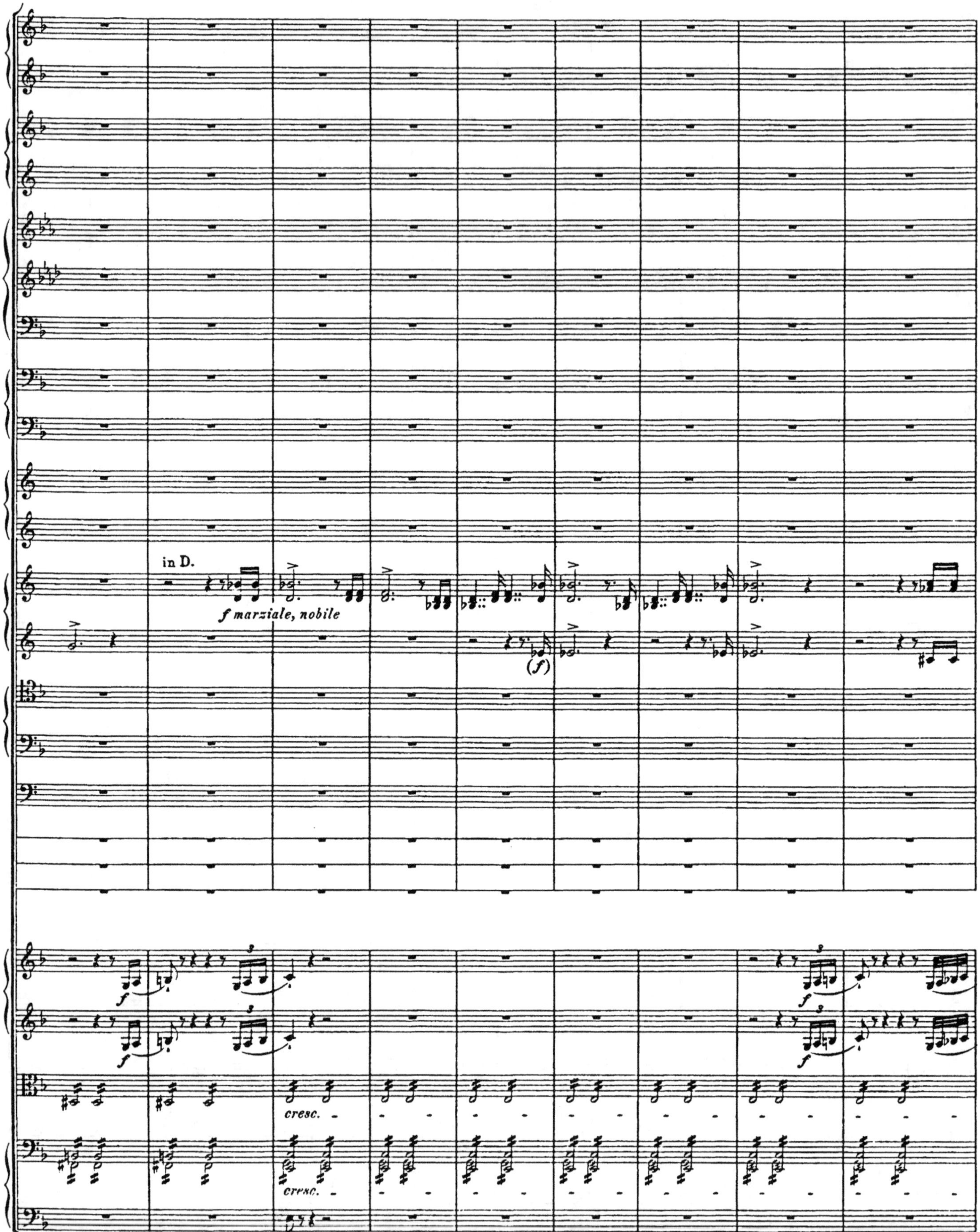
in D.
f marziale, nobile
(f)
cresc.
cresc.

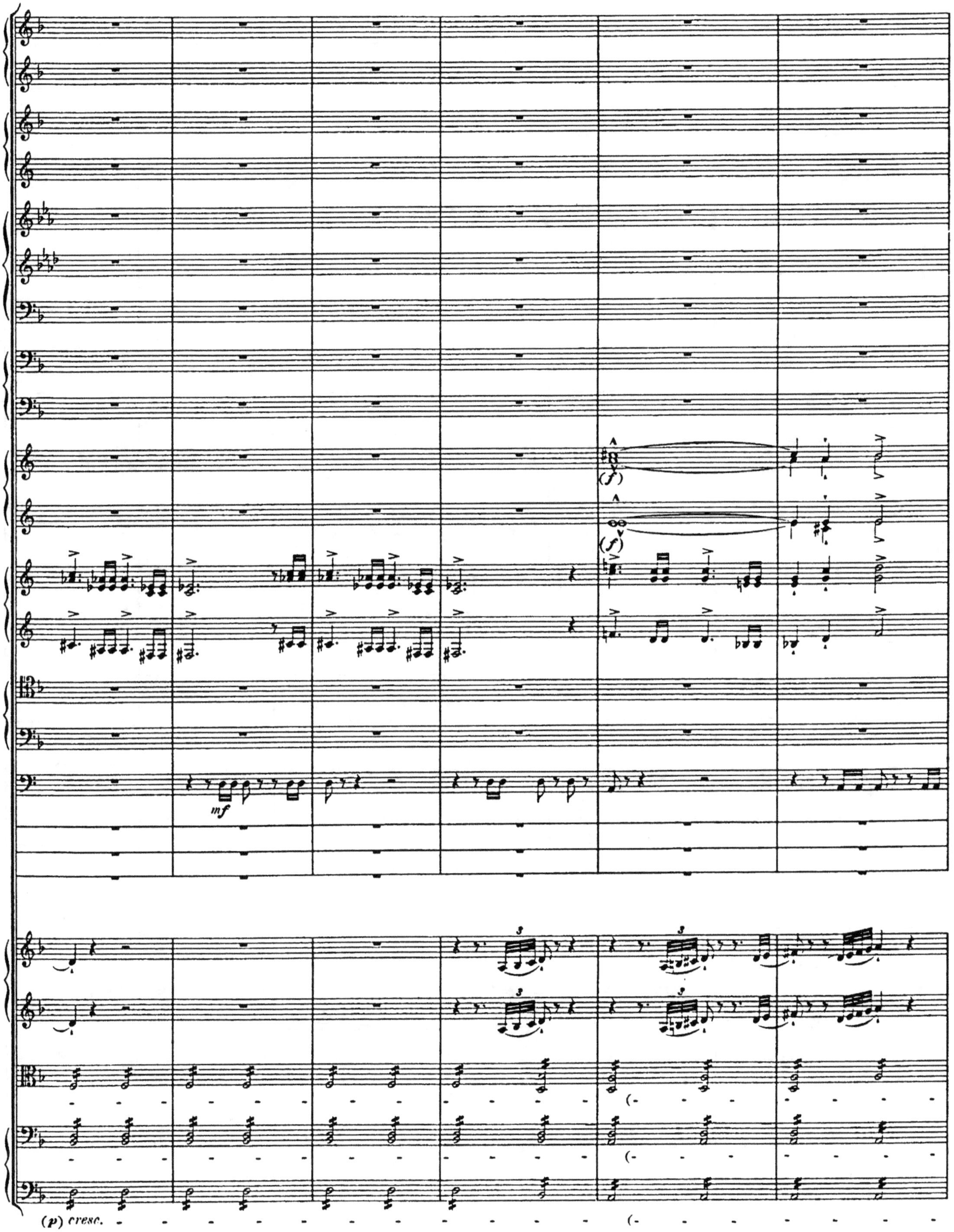
(f)
(f)
mf
3
(p) cresc.

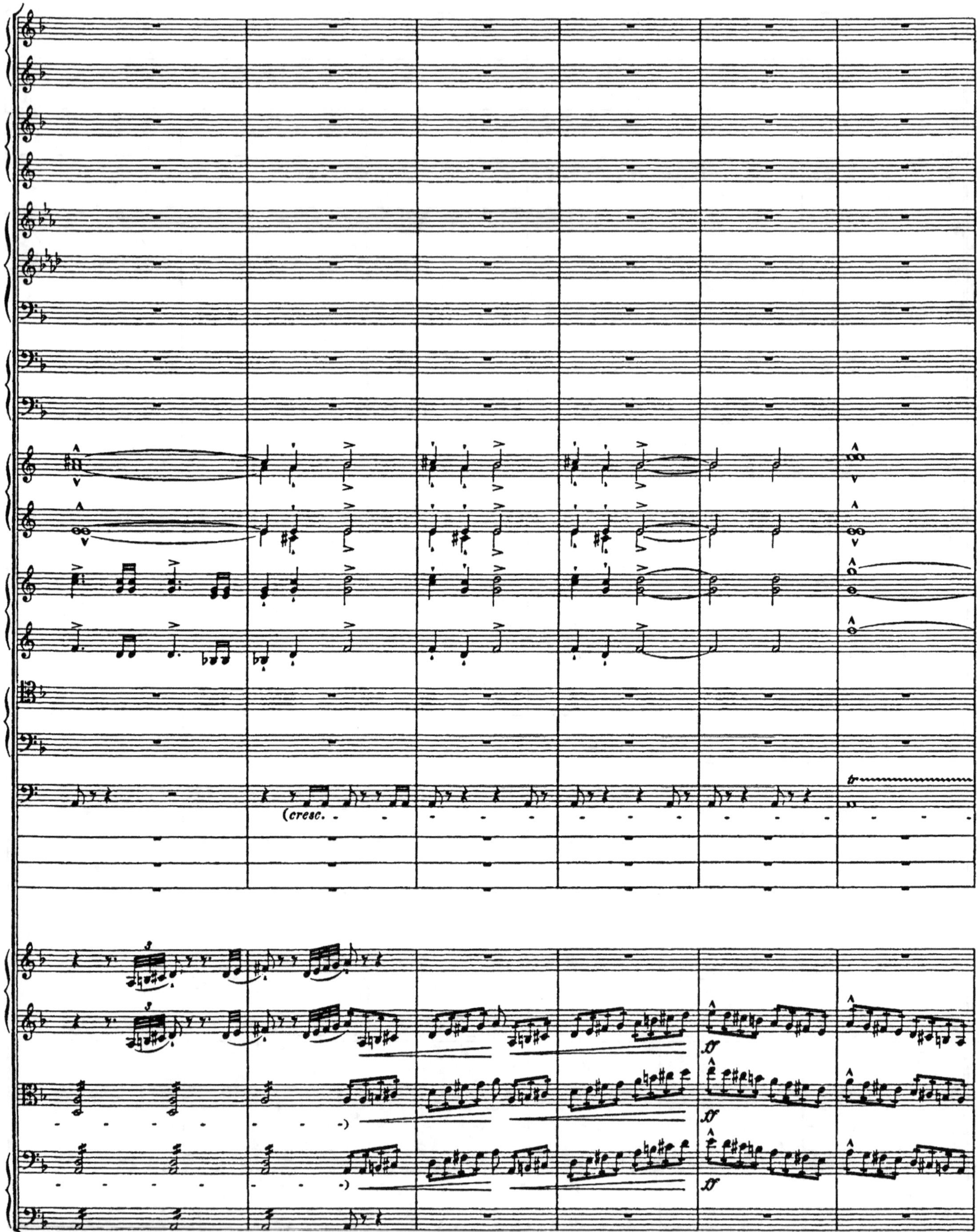
(cresc.
tr
ff
ff
ff

Allegro marziale.

muta in D.

Allegro marziale.

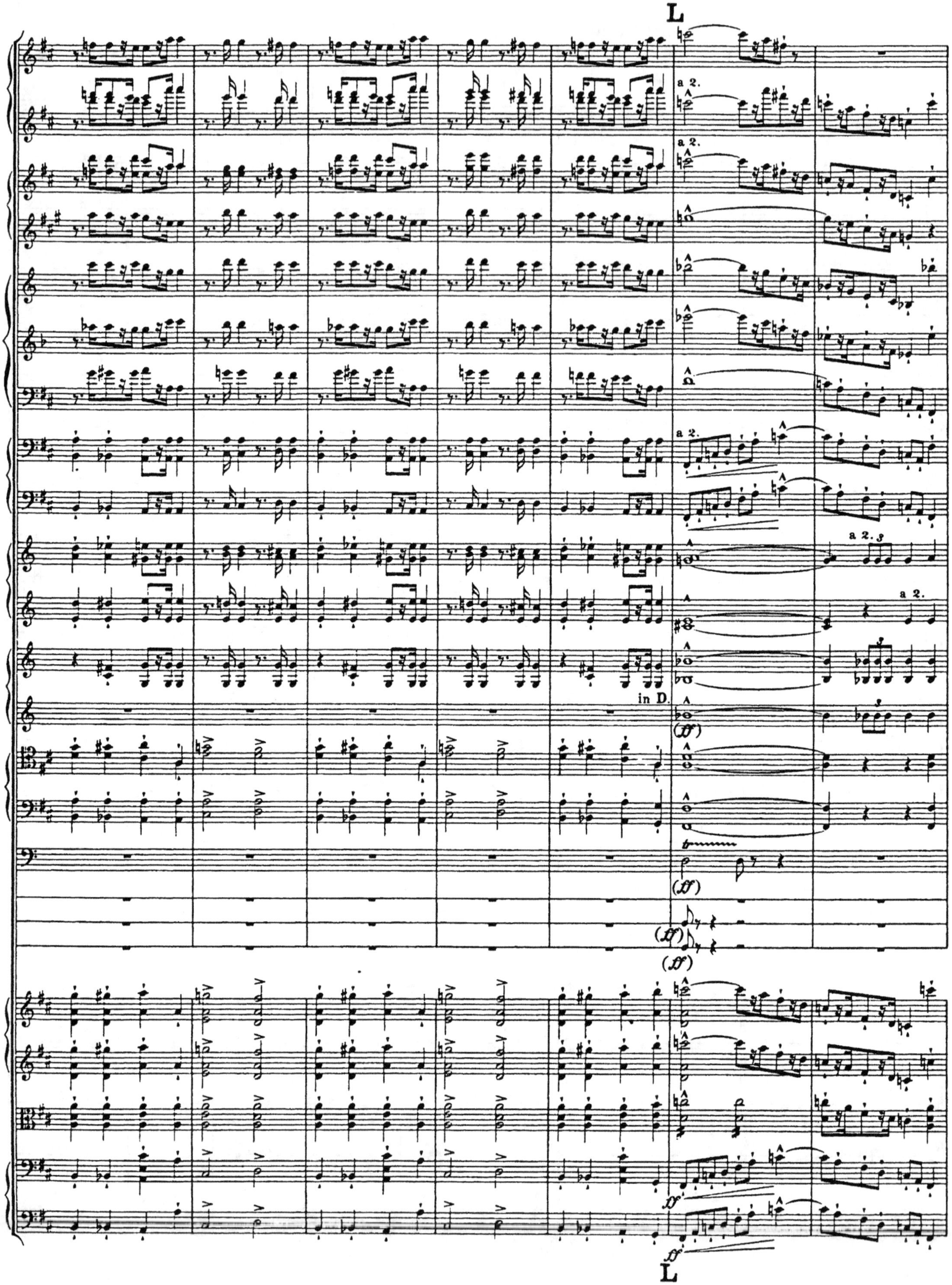
L
a 2.
a 2.
a 2.
a 2. 3
a 2.
in D.
(ff)
(ff)
(ff)
(ff)
ff
ff
L

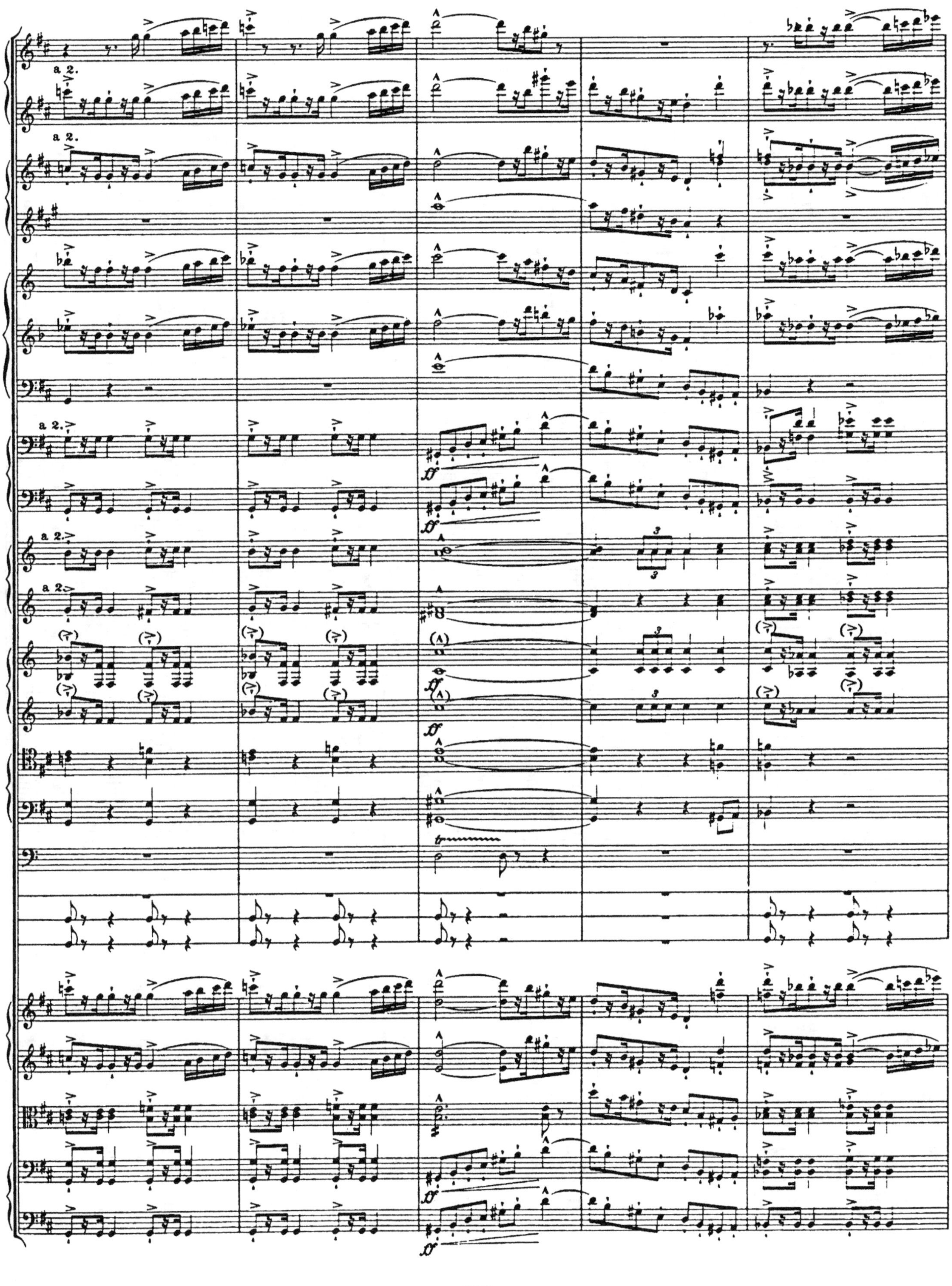
a 2.
a 2.
a 2.
a 2.
a 2.
ff
ff
ff
ff
ff
ff

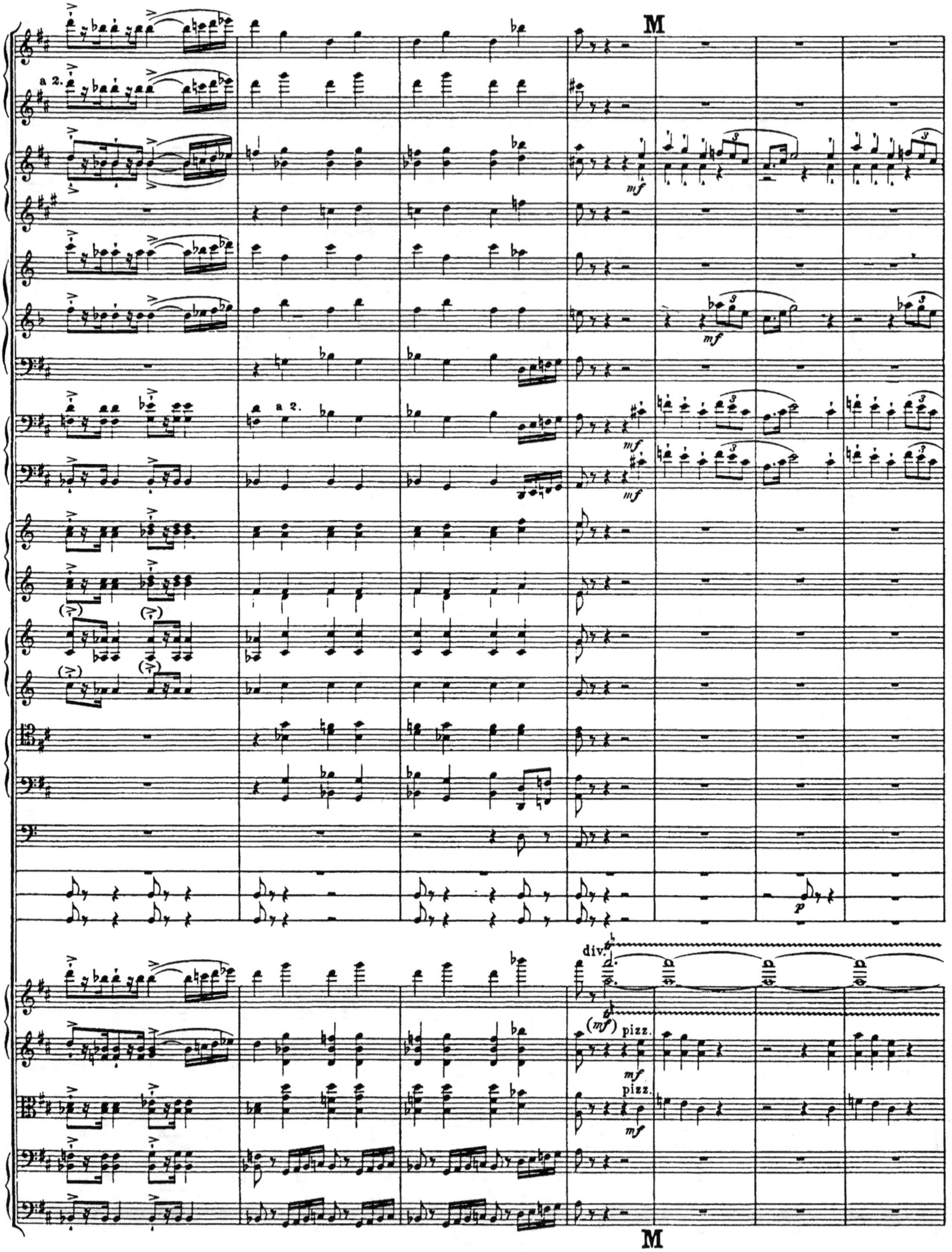
M
a 2.
mf
a 2.
mf
mf
p
div.
(mf)
pizz.
mf
pizz.
mf
M

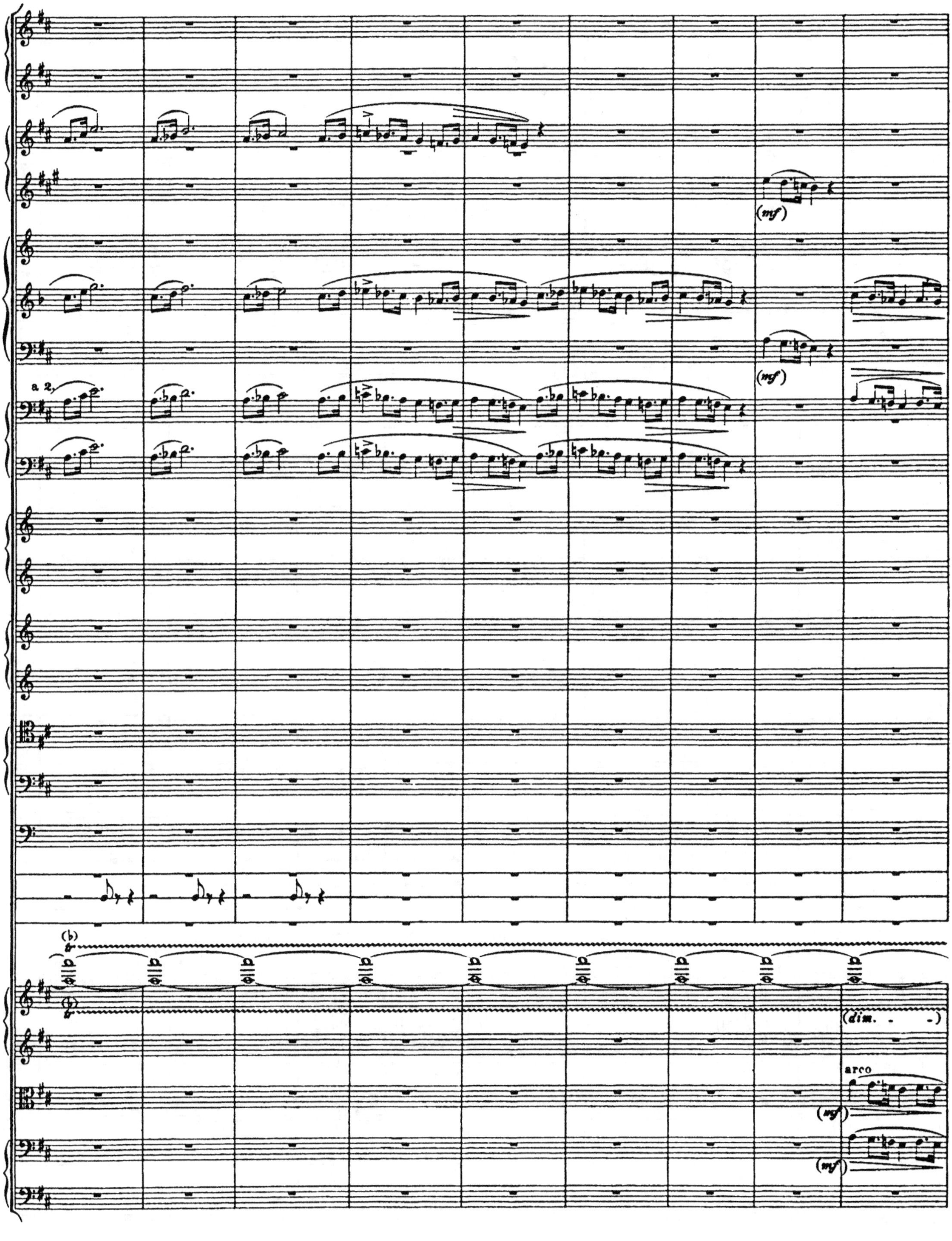
(mf)
a 2.
(mf)
(dim. - -)
arco
(mf)
(mf)

N
a 2.
p
(p)
(p) un poco marc.
(p)
p sempre
(p)
arco
divisi
(p) pizz.
pizz.
(p)
arco
pizz.
N

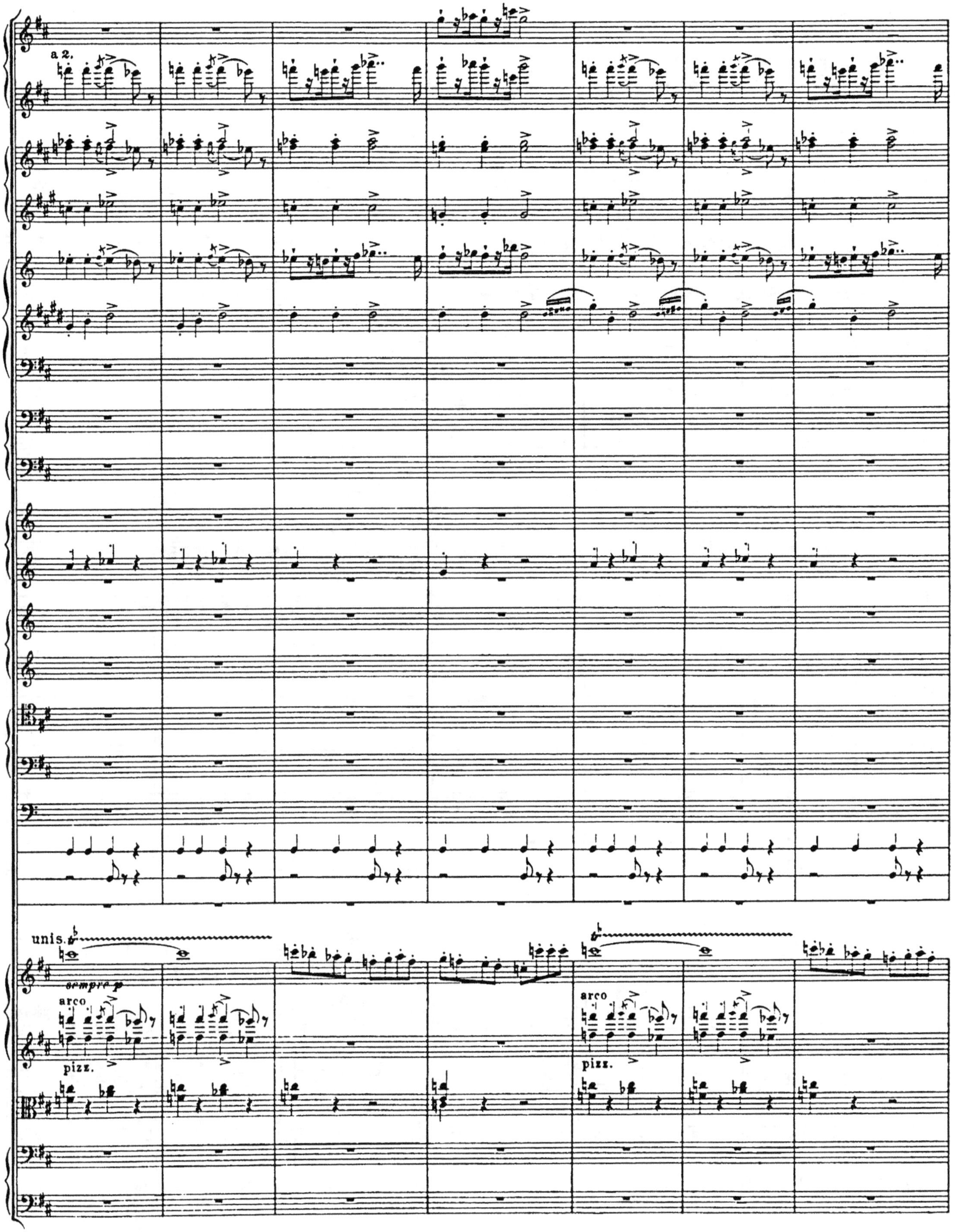
a 2.
unis.
sempre p
arco
pizz.
arco
pizz.

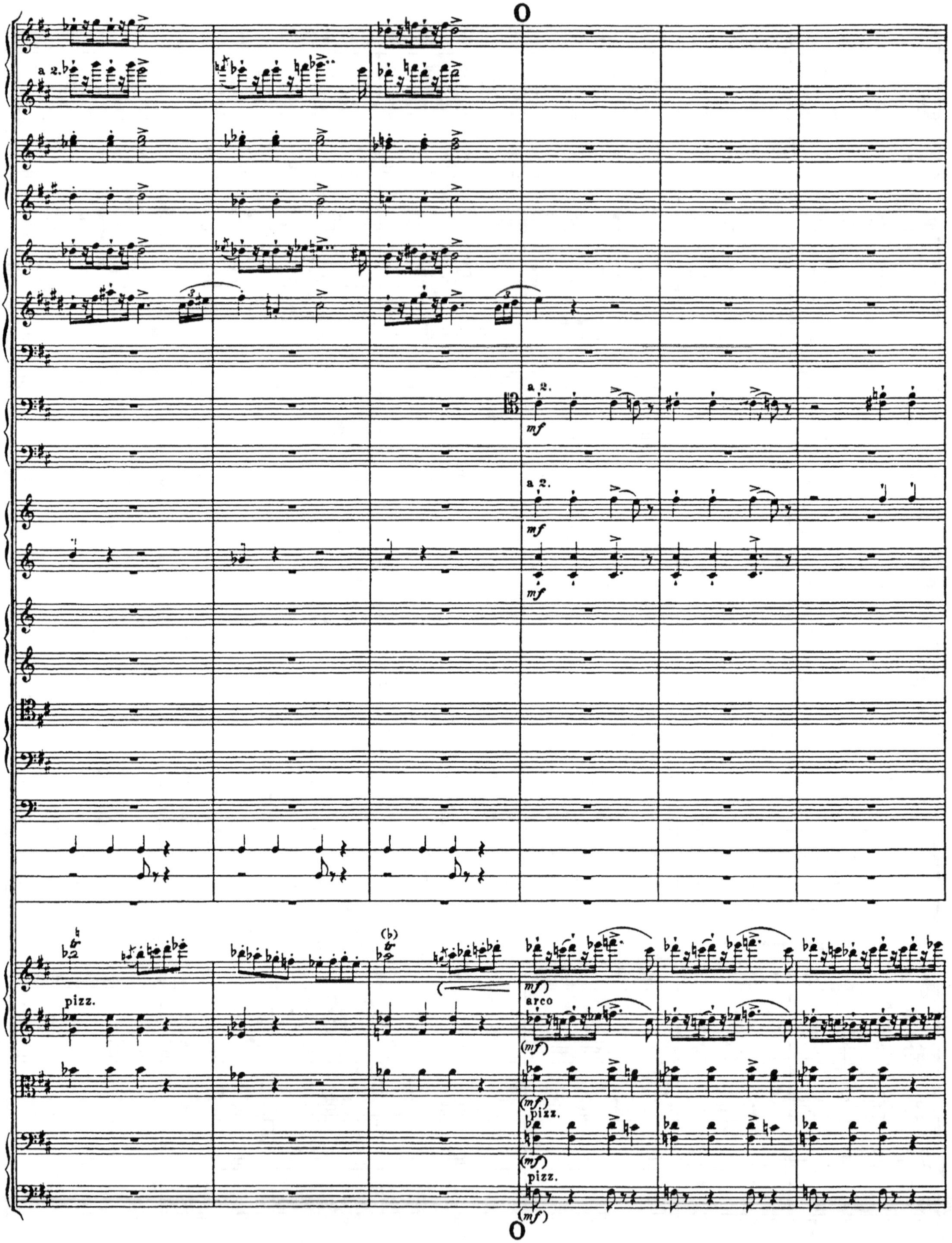
O
a 2.
a 2.
mf
a 2.
mf
mf
pizz.
(b)
(mf)
arco
(mf)
(mf)
pizz.
(mf)
pizz.
(mf)
O

1.
a 2.
mf
mf
(dim)
(p)
dim.
(p)
(p)
ff
ff
ff
p
p
arco
(p)
(p)
(p)
cresc.
cresc.
cresc.
molto
molto
molto
ff
ff
arco
rinf.
ff
arco
ff
1.

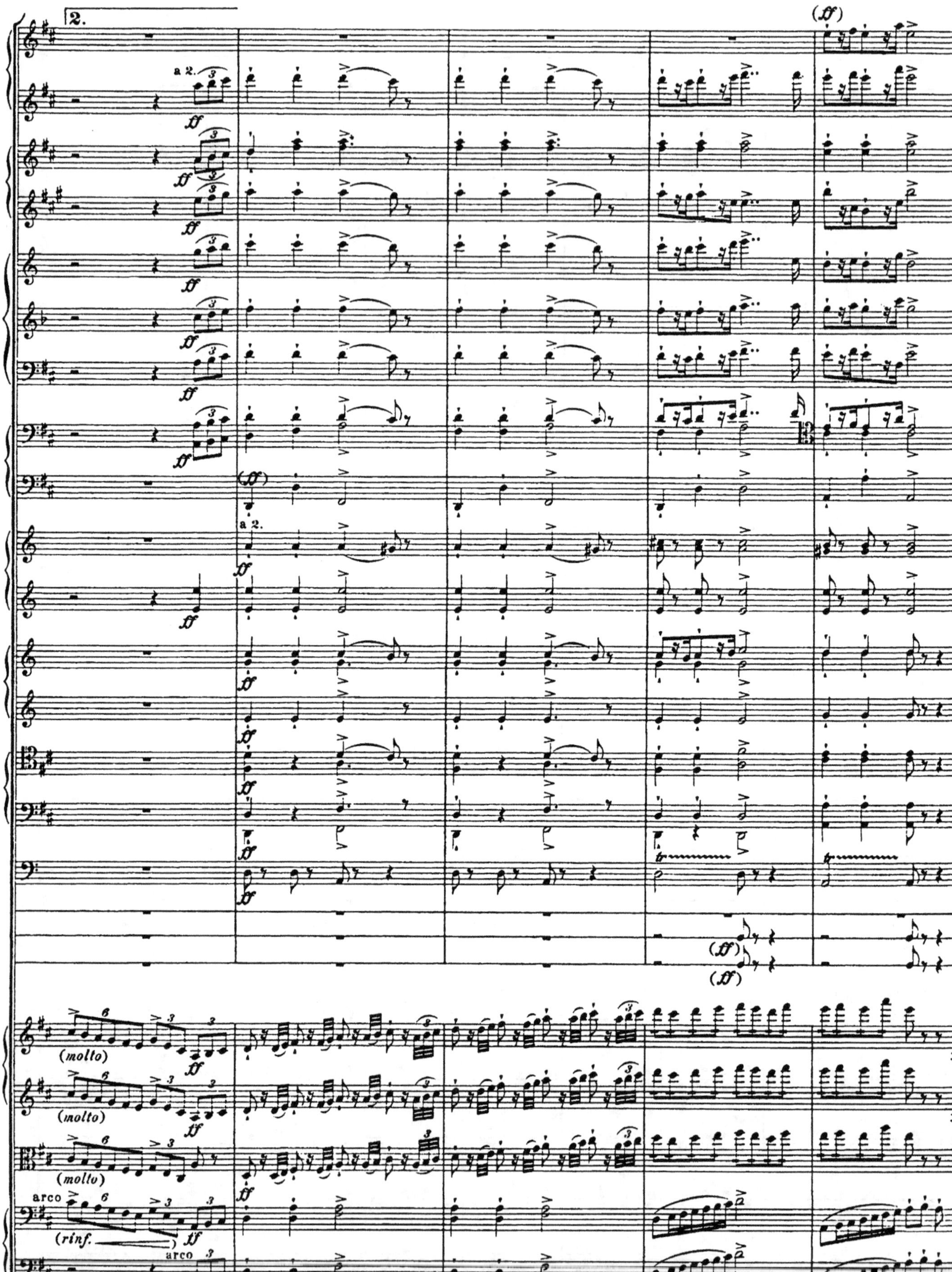
2.
(ff)
a 2.
ff
(molto)
arco
(rinf.
tr
2.

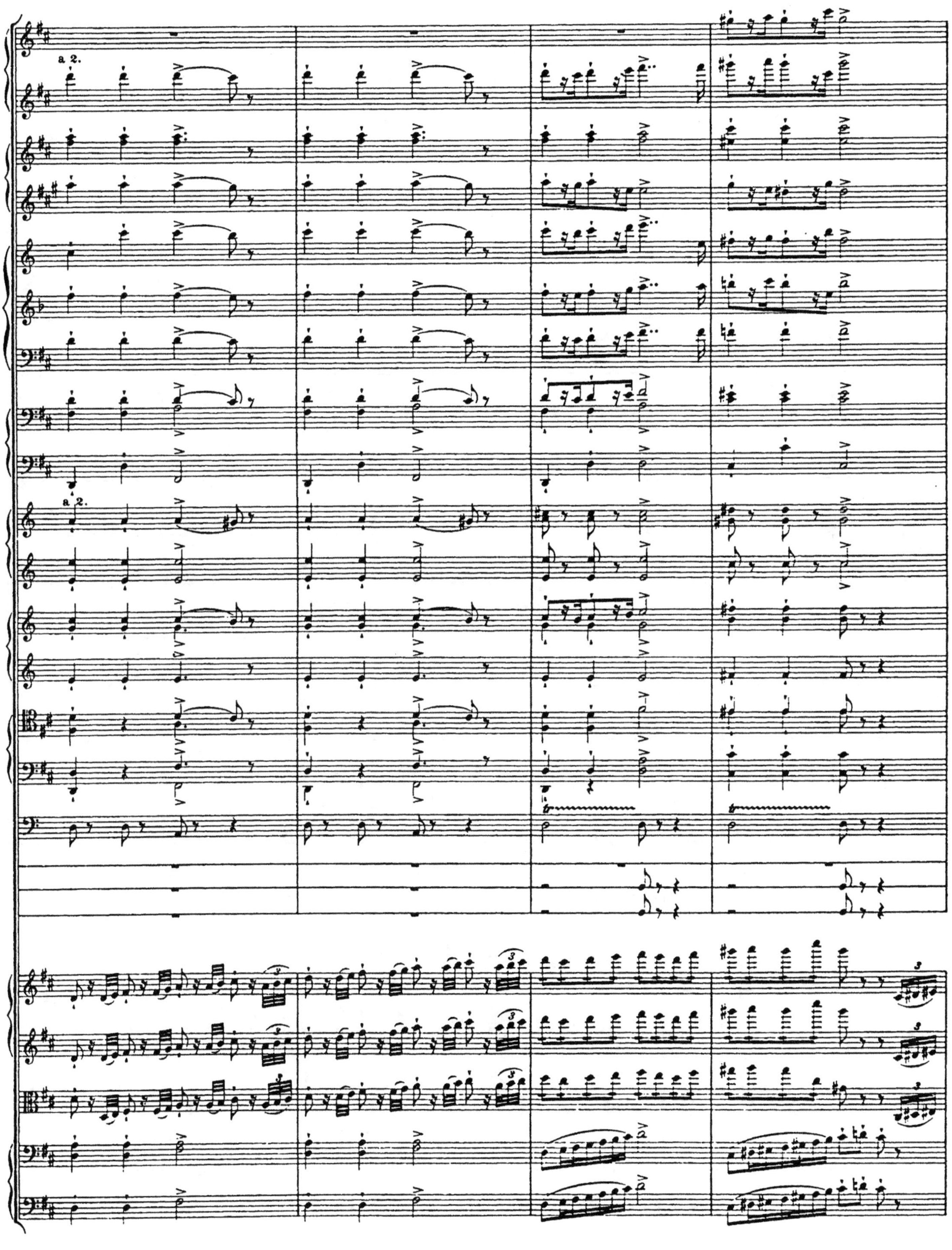
a 2.
a 2.

88

40260

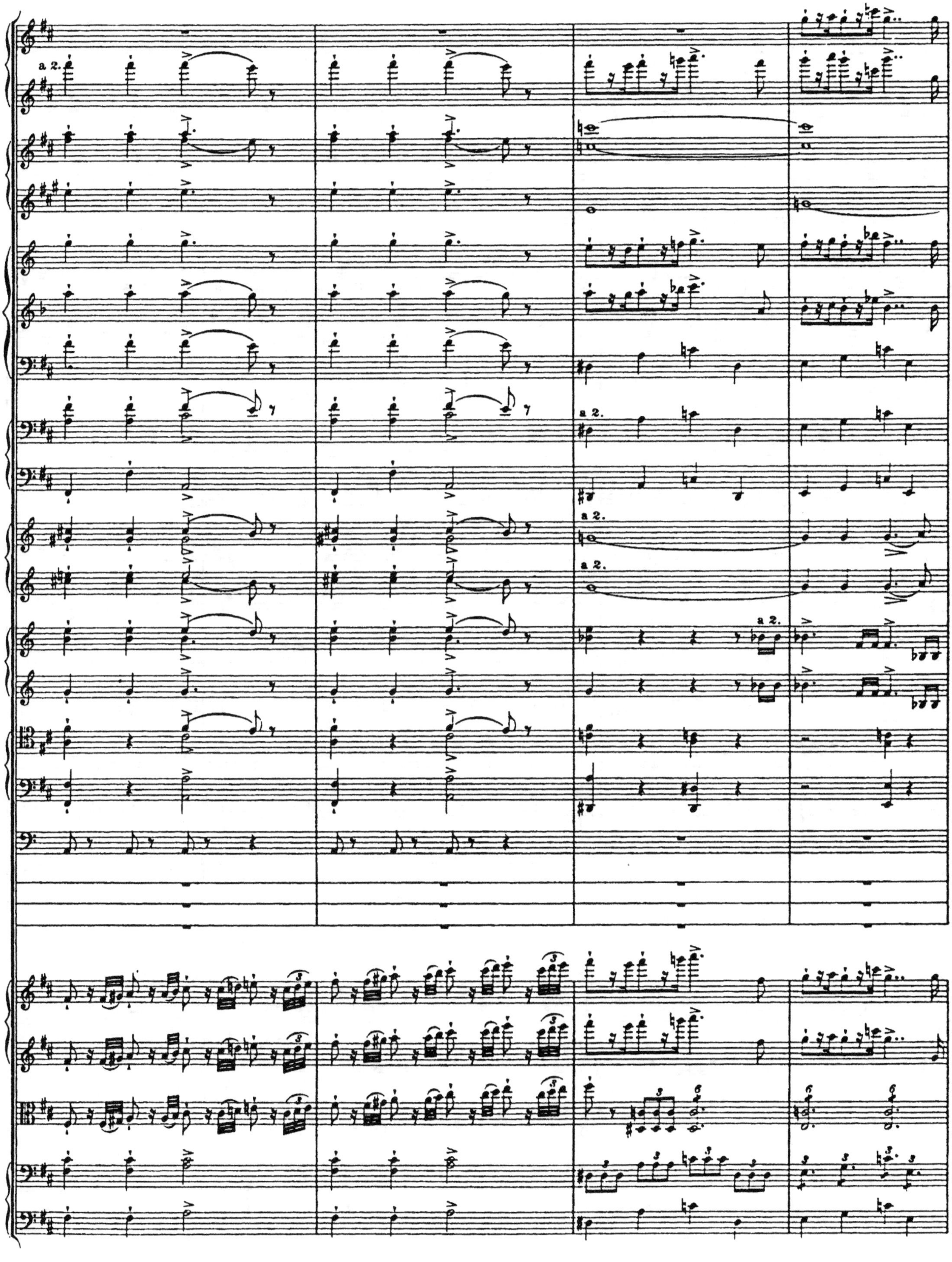
a 2.
a 2.
a 2.
a 2.
a 2.

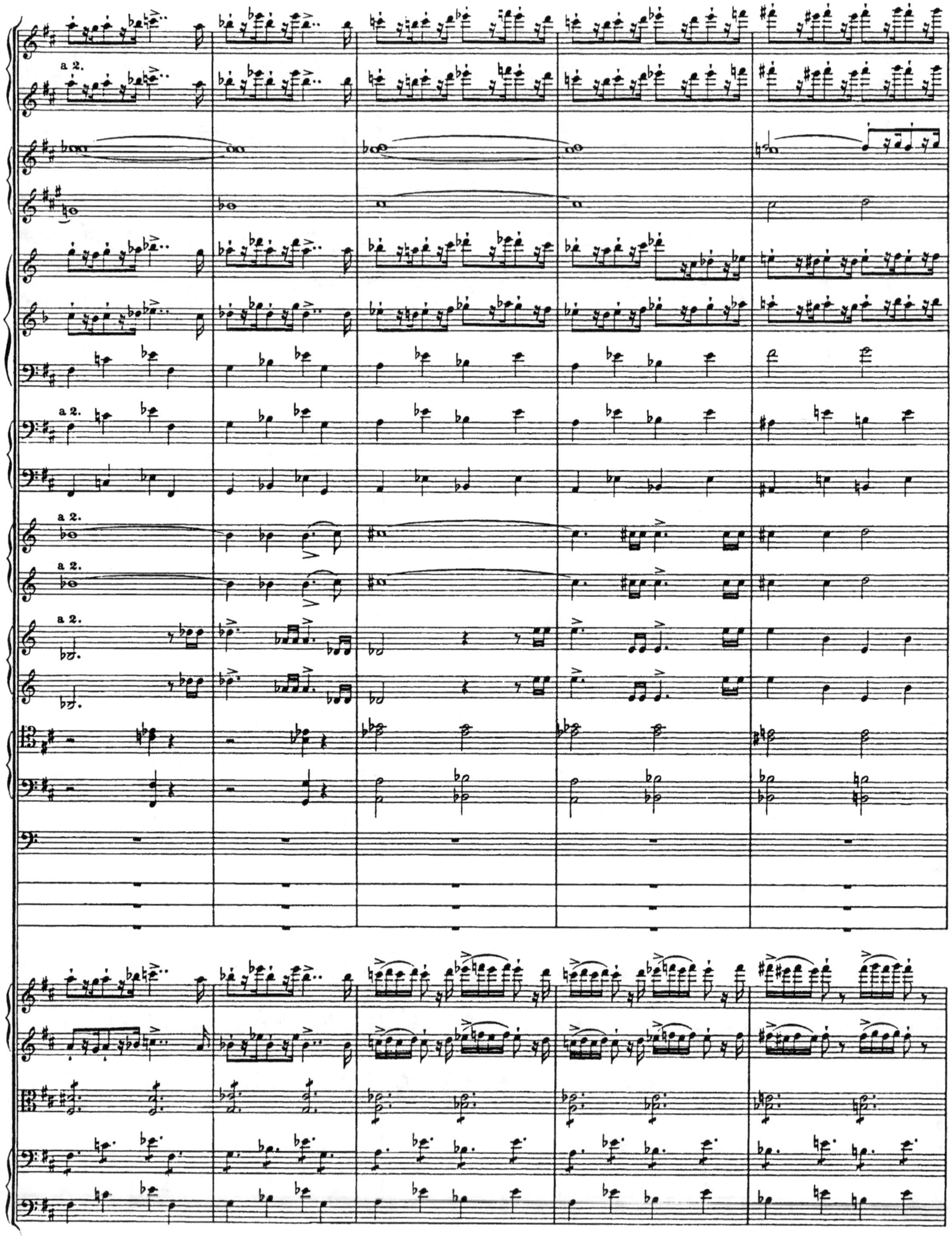
a 2.
a 2.
a 2.
a 2.
a 2.

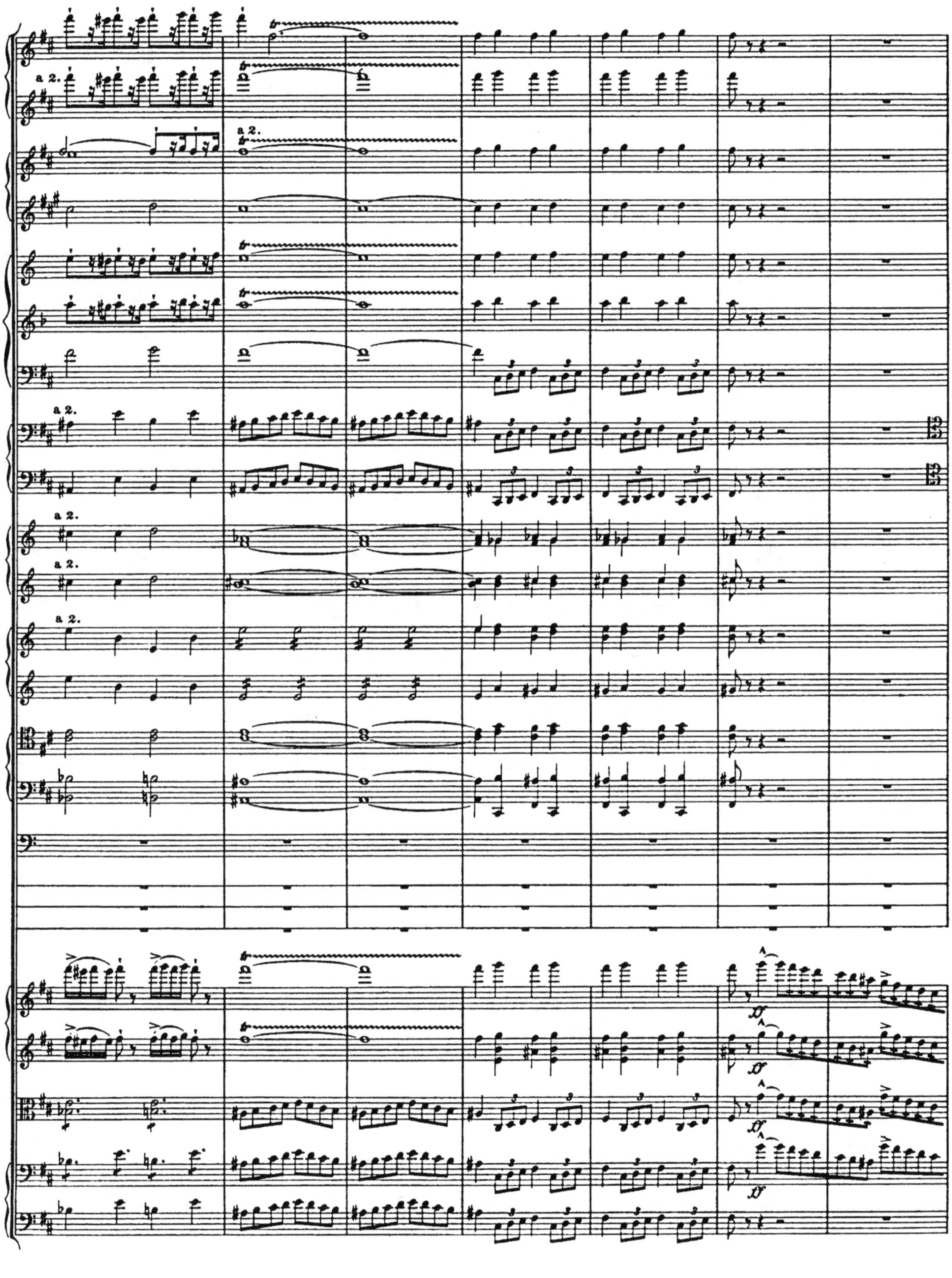
a 2.
a 2.
a 2.
a 2.
a 2.
a 2.
tr
ff

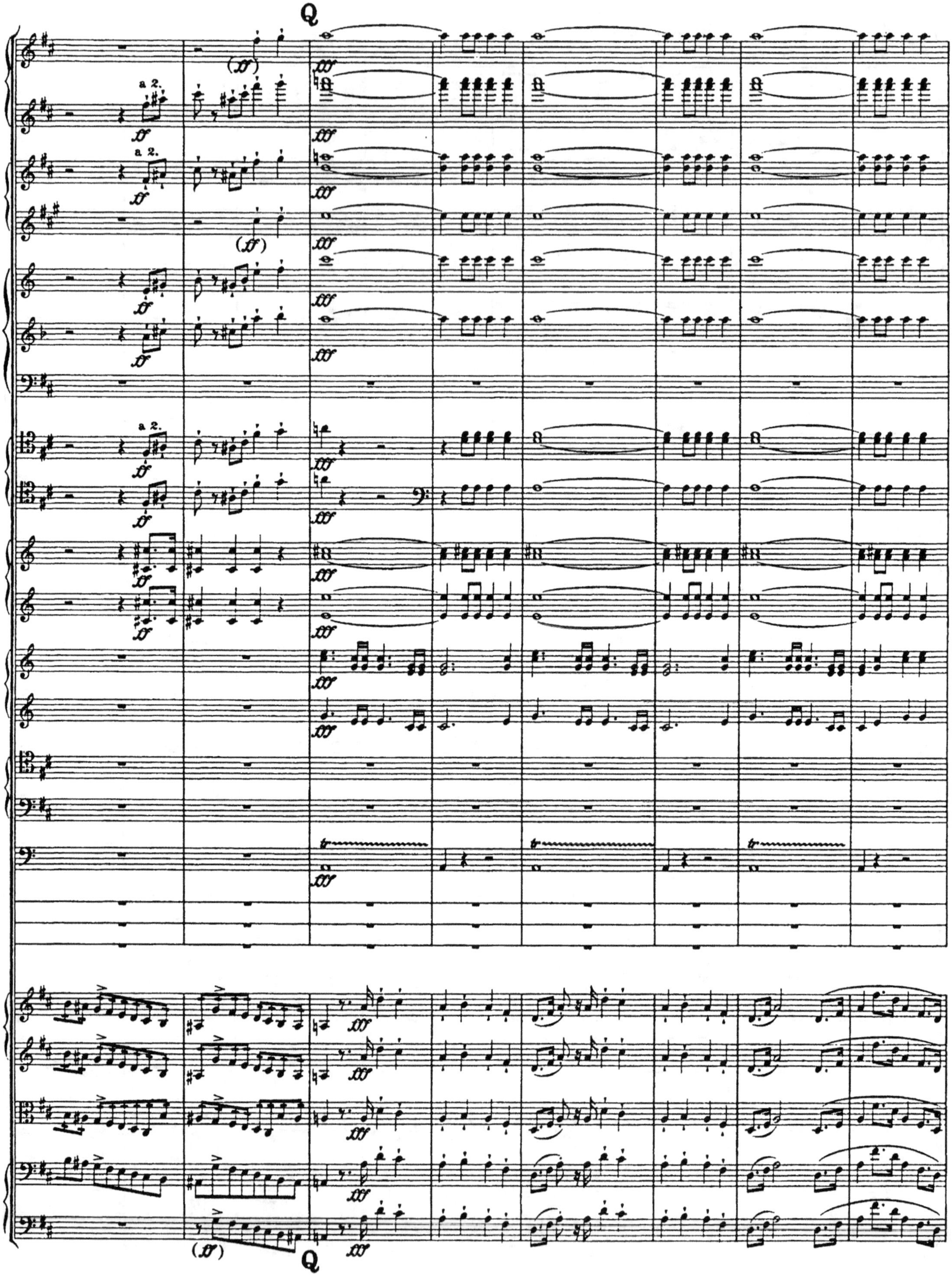
Q
a 2.
a 2.
a 2.
Q

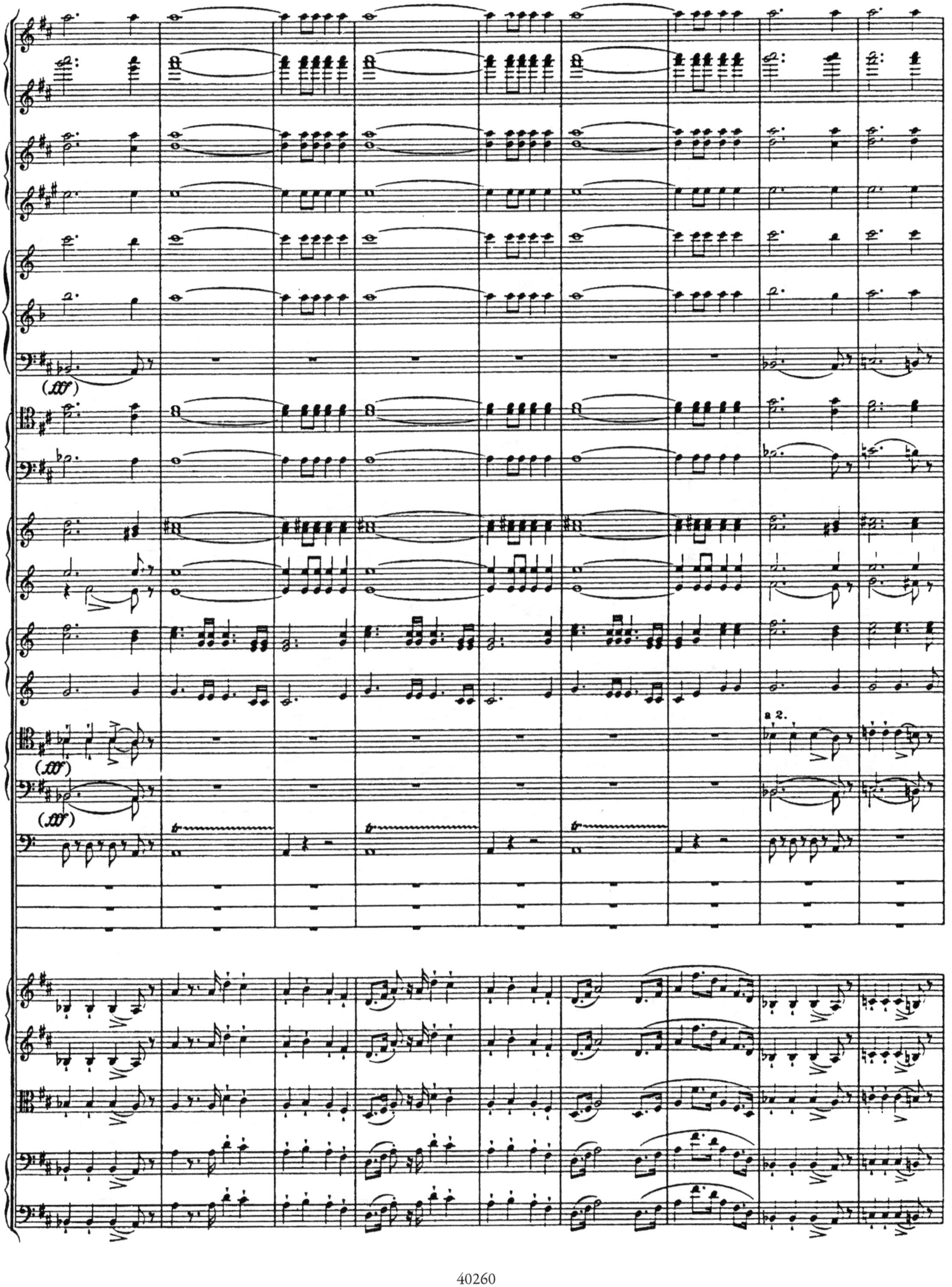
(fff)
(fff)
(fff)
a 2.

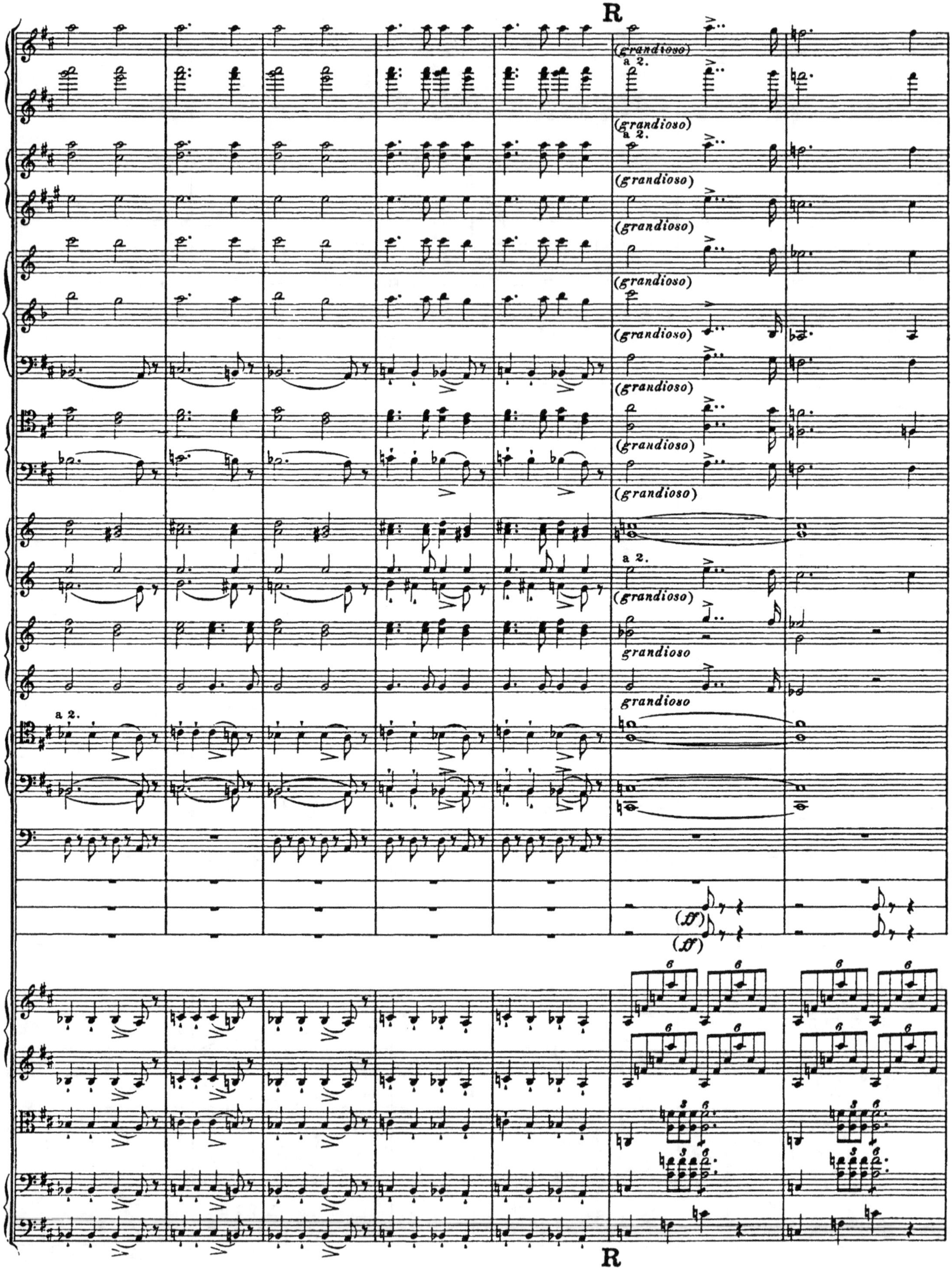
R
(grandioso)
a 2.
grandioso
(ff)
R

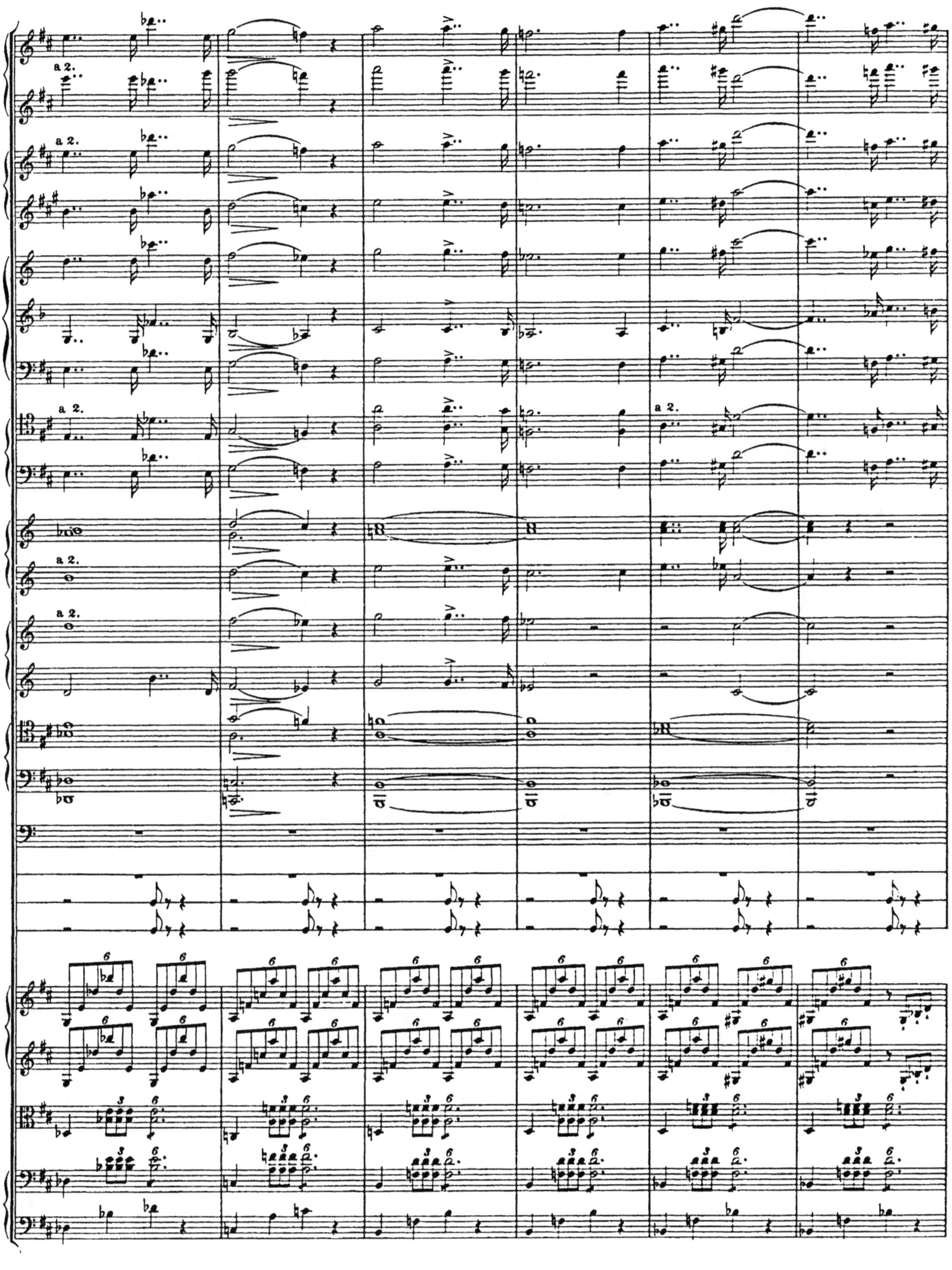
a 2.
a 2.
a 2.
a 2.
a 2.
a 2.

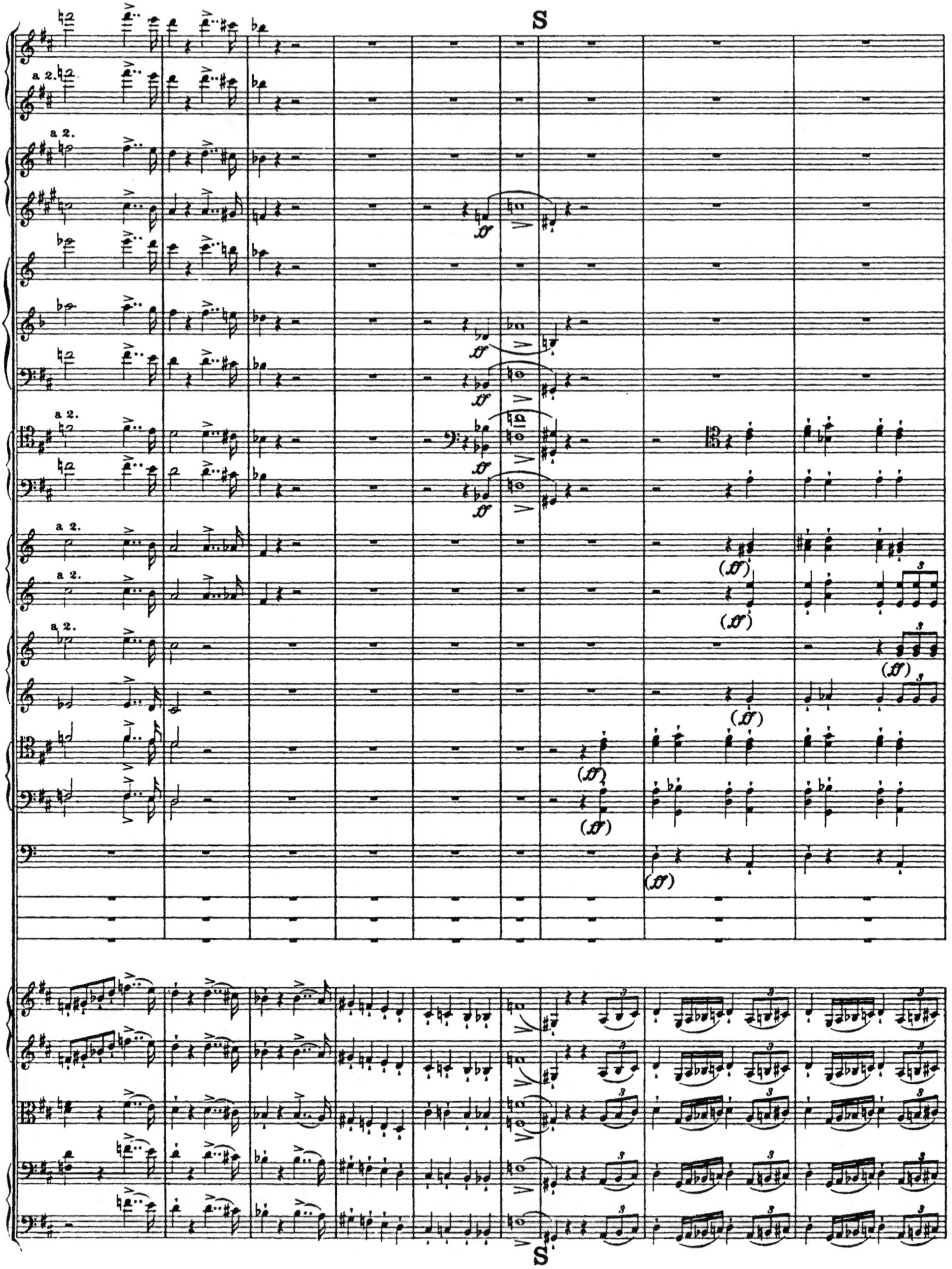
S
a 2.
a 2.
a 2.
a 2.
a 2.
a 2.
ff
(ff)
S

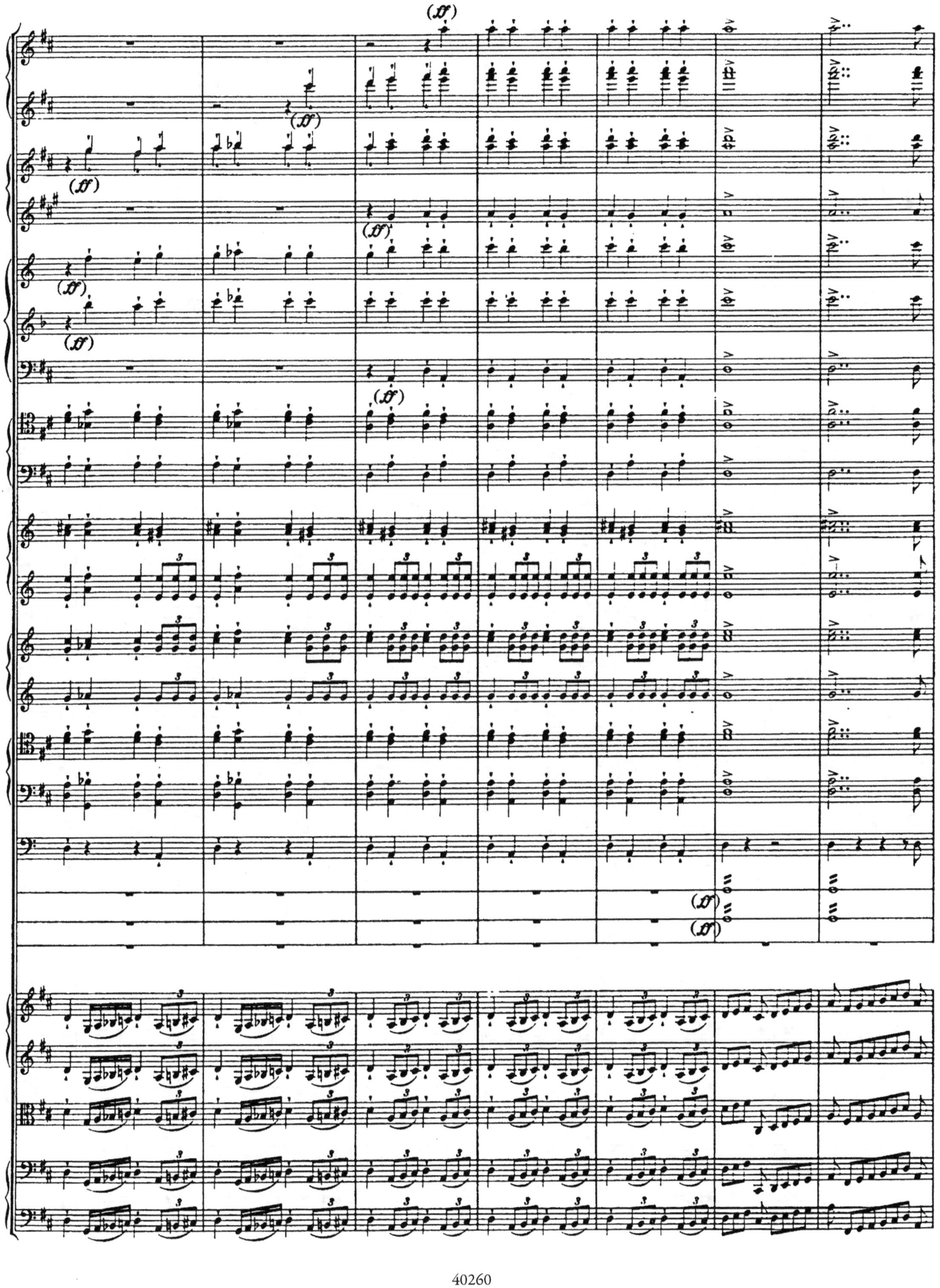
(ff)
(ff)
(ff)
(ff)
(ff)
(ff)
(ff)
(ff)
(ff)

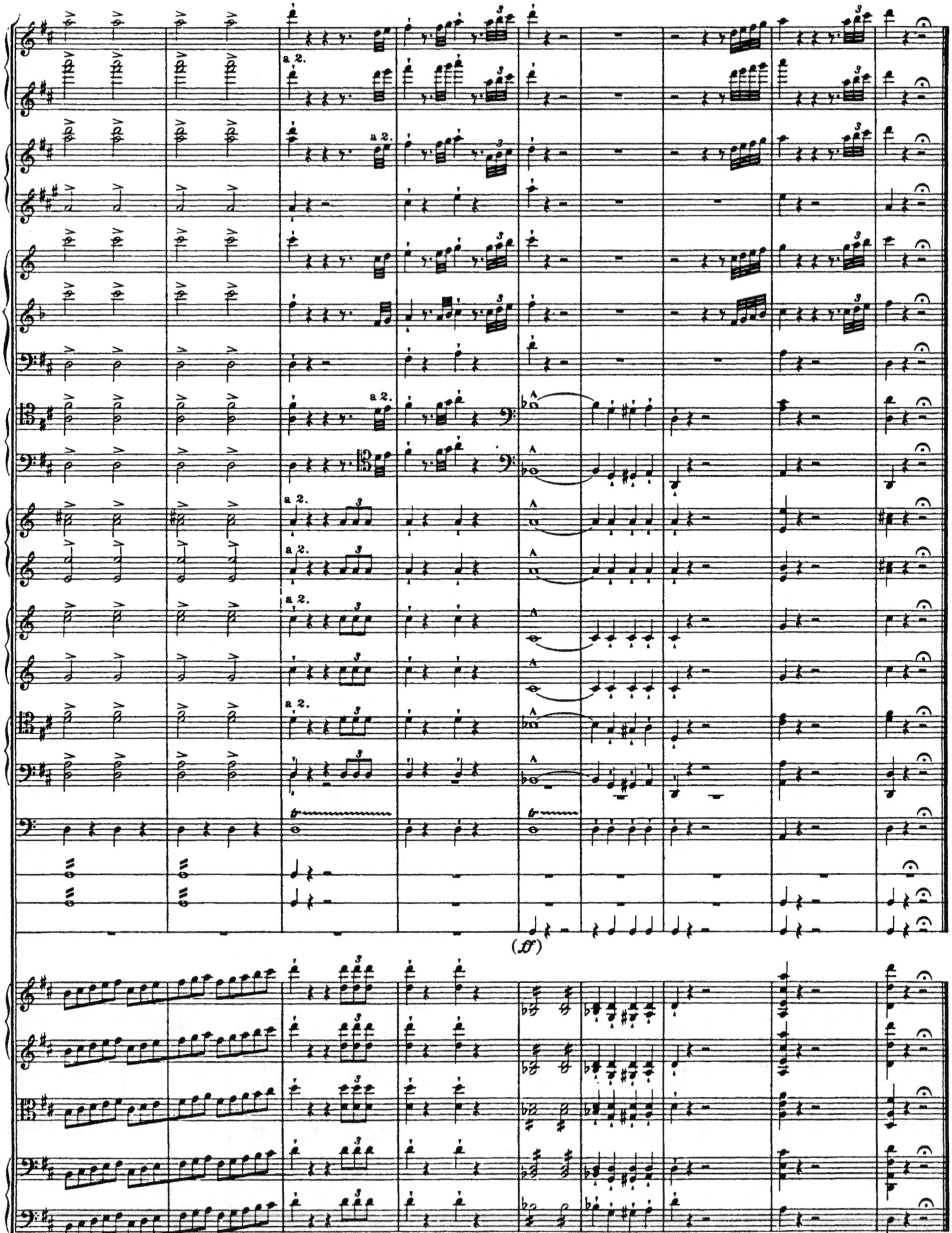
a 2.
a 2.
a 2.
a 2.
a 2.
a 2.
a 2.
tr
tr
(ff)

FRANZ LISZTS
SYMPHONISCHE DICHTUNGEN 5 u. 6

REVISIONSBERICHT

Im Jahre 1908 wurden in einer gemeinschaftlichen Sitzung der Revisoren, der Herausgeber und der Verleger die Leitgedanken und Grundsätze für eine vollständige, einheitliche und korrekte Gesamtausgabe der Werke Franz Liszts beraten und endgültig festgesetzt.

Aus praktischen Gründen der modernen Musikpflege mußten die vielfachen Unterschiede in der Benennung und Anordnung der Instrumente, in den Schlüsseln usw., vor allem aber sehr viele, für heutige Begriffe überflüssige oder selbst störende Versetzungszeichen beseitigt werden. Die auf letztere bezügliche Bestimmung lautet in endgültiger Fassung:

»Die von Liszt sehr reichlich angewendeten zufälligen Versetzungszeichen (namentlich Auflösungszeichen) sind für die heutige Praxis zum Teil entbehrlich geworden. Die nicht unbedingt notwendigen sind nur da beizubehalten, wo sie das Lesen tatsächlich noch erleichtern, Mißverständnisse verhüten oder für das harmonische Bild Lisztscher Schreibweise besonders charakteristisch erscheinen.«

Um jede Willkür auszuschliessen, sind alle irgendwie nennenswerten Änderungen, Weglassungen, Zusätze im Wortlaut der Lisztschen Partitur im Revisionsbericht je bei der betreffenden Komposition besonders aufgeführt und begründet worden, sodaß jeder mit der alten und der neuen Ausgabe in der Hand sich sein Urteil selbst bilden kann. Alle Zutaten, insbesondere Vortragsbezeichnungen, wurden in Klammern ( ) oder [ ] gesetzt; in einzelnen Fällen kann und soll dies nachträglich noch geschehen.

Die Herausgabe der Symphonischen Dichtungen war ursprünglich von Herrn Eugen d'Albert übernommen worden, der jedoch wegen anderweitiger großer Inanspruchnahme zurücktrat, nachdem er den Stich aller 12 Werke nur in erster Lesung hatte beaufsichtigen können. Die genaue Nachprüfung übernahm in dankenswerter Weise Herr Otto Taubmann in Berlin, in stetem Einvernehmen mit dem Kustos des Liszt-Museums, Herrn Hofrat Dr. Obrist, als dem Obmann der Revisionskommission.

BAND 3

PROMETHEUS.

Symphonische Dichtung Nr. 5.

Vorlage: Die erste Partiturausgabe, erschienen 1856 bei Breitkopf & Härtel in Leipzig. Verlagsnummer 9191.

Bemerkungen:

S. 9. Die gedruckte Vorlage hat im ersten Takt auf dem dritten Taktviertel in der zweiten Hälfte der II. Violinen die Note d, die als Fehler zu erachten ist; die Fortschreitung ergibt falsche Oktaven mit dem Baß. Es dürfte, wie ein Vergleich mit der analogen Stelle auf S. 41, Takt 3 ergibt, ein Stichfehler vorliegen, der durch Änderung des d in h beseitigt wurde.

S. 44, Takt 4 haben die II. Violinen in der gedruckten Vorlage vom 6. bis zum 8. Achtel ein Diminuendozeichen ($\textgreater$), die rhythmisch mitgehenden Violoncelle und Bässe über der Viertelnote aber nur ein Marcatozeichen ($\cdot$). Da bei der analogen Stelle auf S. 9, 2. Takt auch in den II. Violinen nur das Marcatozeichen steht, wurde $\textgreater$ auf S. 44 als Stichfehler der Vorlage erachtet und in ein Marcatozeichen umgeändert.

S. 51 hat die gedruckte Vorlage im 6. bis 8. Takt für die zusammengehenden Fagotte und 1. Horn verschiedene dynamische Vorschriften, die in Übereinstimmung mit einander gebracht wurden.

* * *

MAZEPPA.

Symphonische Dichtung Nr. 6.

Vorlage: Die erste Partiturausgabe, erschienen 1856 bei Breitkopf & Härtel in Leipzig. Verlagsnummer 9137.

Bemerkungen:

S. 8, 4. Takt
S. 9, 2. u. 4. Takt $\big\}$ wurden die $\textless$ unter den Bläsern auf gleiche Länge mit denen unter den Streichern gebracht.

S. 9, 2. Takt hat die D-Klarinette in der gedruckten Vorlage ais, während b sowohl der Vorzeichnung wie der Stimmführung (as-b-c) nach als viel natürlicher erscheint. Wurde demgemäß geändert.

S. 18, 1. u. 2. Takt wurde das $\textgreater$ in Fagotten, Hörnern und Posaunen gemäß der analogen Stelle auf S. 17, 1. und 2. Takt, bis zum angebundenen Achtel verlängert.

S. 34, 1. Takt ff. und S. 43, 1. Takt ff. ist in der gedruckten Vorlage die Bezeichnung der Violoncellstimmen zweifelhaft. Unter den Triolen des 3. Viertels steht (gleichzeitig mit der entsprechenden Bezeichnung in der zweiten Hälfte der II. Violinen und in den Bratschen) »col legno«. Da die Bezeichnung nicht wiederholt wird, würde sie bis zur Aufhebung ihrer Bedeutung durch eine andere Vorschrift in Geltung zu bleiben haben. Dem widerspricht aber, daß das erste Viertel im ersten dieser Takte nicht »col legno« gespielt werden soll. Da nun die nächsten Takte eine ständige Wiederholung des rhythmischen Motivs

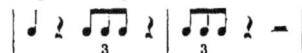

bringen, wurde angenommen, daß es der Absicht des Komponisten entspreche, wenn stets nur die beiden Triolen »col legno«, das vorangehende Viertel aber jedesmal mit Bogenstrich gegeben werde.

S. 58, 7. Takt
S. 59, 1., 3., 5., 7. Takt $\big\}$ Die Zeichen $\times\times$ über den Akkorden in den Streichern bedeuten, laut diesbezüglichen Anmerkungen in den Orchesterstimmen, daß diese Akkorde *pizzicato* gespielt werden sollen.
S. 60, 1., 3. Takt

* * *

www.ingramcontent.com/pod-product-compliance
Lightning Source LLC
LaVergne TN
LVHW081319060426
835509LV00015B/1582